From Neglect to Nurturing: A Journey Towards Self-Care

Patrick Joe

Copyright © [2023]

Title: From Neglect to Nurturing: A Journey Towards Self-Care
Author's: Patrick Joe

All rights reserved. No part of this publication may be reproduced, stored in a retrieval system, or transmitted in any form or by any means, electronic, mechanical, photocopying, recording, or otherwise, without the prior written permission of the publisher or author, except in the case of brief quotations embodied in critical reviews and certain other non-commercial uses permitted by copyright law.

This book was printed and published by [Publisher's: **Patrick Joe**] in [2023]

ISBN:

TABLE OF CONTENT

Chapter 1: The Importance of Self-Care — 08

Understanding Self-Care

Defining Self-Care

Recognizing the Different Aspects of Self-Care

The Neglect of Self-Care

Society's Influence on Neglecting Self-Care

Personal Factors Contributing to Neglecting Self-Care

Consequences of Neglecting Self-Care

Physical Consequences

Mental and Emotional Consequences

Social and Relationship Consequences

Chapter 2: Exploring the Journey 28

Acknowledging the Need for Self-Care

Recognizing the Signs of Neglecting Self-Care

Understanding the Importance of Prioritizing Self-Care

Overcoming Barriers to Self-Care

Identifying Internal Barriers

Addressing External Barriers

Building a Foundation for Self-Care

Setting Personal Boundaries

Establishing Healthy Habits and Routines

Chapter 3: Self-Care Practices 46

Physical Self-Care

Nurturing Your Body Through Exercise

Prioritizing Nutrition for Optimal Well-Being

Emotional Self-Care

Practicing Mindfulness and Meditation

Engaging in Creative Outlets for Emotional Expression

Mental Self-Care

Cultivating a Positive Mindset

Engaging in Continuous Learning and Growth

Social Self-Care

Building and Maintaining Supportive Relationships

Setting Healthy Boundaries in Social Interactions

Chapter 4: Overcoming Challenges   70

Dealing with Guilt and Self-Sabotage

Recognizing and Challenging Guilt

Overcoming Self-Sabotaging Thoughts and Behaviors

Overcoming Time Constraints

Prioritizing Self-Care in a Busy Schedule

Finding Creative Ways to Make Time for Self-Care

Seeking Support and Accountability

Identifying Sources of Support

Creating Accountability Systems

Chapter 5: Sustaining Self-Care Practices   88

Creating a Self-Care Plan

Setting Realistic Goals

Designing a Personalized Self-Care Routine

Cultivating Resilience and Adaptability

Embracing Change and Uncertainty

Developing Coping Mechanisms for Stressful Situations

Celebrating Self-Care Victories

Recognizing and Acknowledging Progress

Rewarding Yourself for Consistent Self-Care Efforts

Conclusion: Embracing a Life of Self-Care   106

Chapter 1: The Importance of Self-Care

Understanding Self-Care

In today's fast-paced and demanding world, taking care of ourselves often takes a backseat to our numerous responsibilities and commitments. We find ourselves caught up in the never-ending cycle of work, family, and social obligations, neglecting the most important person in our lives - ourselves. This subchapter aims to shed light on the significance of self-care and its impact on our overall well-being.

Self-care is not a luxury, but a necessity. It involves deliberately taking the time to prioritize our physical, mental, and emotional health. It encompasses activities that rejuvenate and replenish our energy, allowing us to function at our best. However, self-care goes beyond indulging in occasional pampering sessions; it is a holistic approach to nurturing oneself on a regular basis.

One of the primary reasons why self-care is essential is its effect on our mental health. Neglecting self-care can lead to increased stress levels, anxiety, and even burnout. By engaging in activities that promote relaxation and stress reduction, such as meditation, exercise, or pursuing hobbies, we can improve our mental well-being, enhance our resilience, and better cope with life's challenges.

Furthermore, self-care plays a crucial role in maintaining physical health. It involves adopting healthy lifestyle choices such as regular exercise, balanced nutrition, and sufficient sleep. By prioritizing our physical well-being, we can prevent chronic diseases and boost our immune system, enabling us to lead a more fulfilling and active life.

Self-care is also closely linked to our emotional well-being. It involves acknowledging and addressing our emotions, establishing healthy boundaries, and seeking support when needed. By practicing self-compassion and self-acceptance, we can foster a positive self-image and improve our relationships with others.

Understanding the importance of self-care is the first step towards incorporating it into our daily lives. It is not a selfish act but an act of self-love and self-preservation. By taking care of ourselves, we become better equipped to care for others and fulfill our responsibilities effectively. It allows us to recharge and refuel, preventing feelings of overwhelm and exhaustion.

In conclusion, self-care is an indispensable component of a healthy and fulfilling life. By consciously making self-care a priority, we can enhance our overall well-being, both physically and mentally. It empowers us to take control of our lives and cultivate a harmonious balance between our responsibilities and personal needs. So, let us embark on this journey towards self-care, where neglect is replaced by nurturing, and we can thrive in every aspect of our lives.

Defining Self-Care

Self-care is an essential aspect of maintaining overall well-being, yet it is often overlooked or neglected in the hustle and bustle of everyday life. In this subchapter, we will explore the concept of self-care and highlight its importance in our lives.

Self-care can be defined as the practice of taking deliberate actions to promote physical, mental, and emotional well-being. It involves consciously attending to one's own needs and prioritizing activities that bring joy, relaxation, and rejuvenation. It is not a luxury, but a necessity for leading a fulfilling life.

In today's fast-paced world, many individuals find themselves caught up in the demands of work, relationships, and various responsibilities. They often forget to allocate time and energy for themselves, leading to burnout, stress, and a decline in overall health. This is where self-care becomes imperative.

Self-care encompasses a wide range of activities that can be tailored to suit individual preferences. It may involve engaging in hobbies, practicing mindfulness or meditation, spending quality time with loved ones, or simply taking a break from the constant demands of daily life. It is crucial to note that self-care is not selfish; it is an act of self-preservation, allowing us to recharge and show up fully in all aspects of our lives.

Recognizing the impotence of self-care is essential. It is not just about pampering oneself with occasional treats or indulgences; it is about establishing healthy habits and routines that support our overall well-being. Self-care is not a one-size-fits-all approach; it requires self-reflection and awareness to determine what activities and practices resonate with us individually.

By prioritizing self-care, we can counteract the negative effects of stress, improve our mental and emotional resilience, and enhance our relationships with others. It enables us to become more present, compassionate, and empathetic towards ourselves and others. Moreover, self-care fosters personal growth and self-discovery, allowing us to tap into our true potential.

In the subsequent chapters, we will delve deeper into various aspects of self-care, exploring different strategies, techniques, and practices that can be incorporated into our daily lives. Remember, self-care is not a destination but a journey. It requires consistent effort, self-compassion, and a commitment to nurturing ourselves. So, let us embark on this transformative journey together and reclaim our well-being through the power of self-care.

Recognizing the Different Aspects of Self-Care

In our fast-paced and demanding world, it is easy to neglect our own needs and well-being. We often prioritize work, family, and other responsibilities, forgetting to take care of ourselves. However, self-care is not just a luxury; it is a necessity for our physical, emotional, and mental health. To truly nurture ourselves, we must recognize the different aspects of self-care and their importance in our lives.

Physical self-care is the foundation of overall well-being. It involves taking care of our bodies through regular exercise, nourishing our bodies with nutritious food, getting enough sleep, and addressing any physical ailments or discomforts. By prioritizing our physical health, we can increase our energy levels, boost our immune system, and improve our overall quality of life.

Emotional self-care is equally crucial. It involves acknowledging and validating our emotions, expressing them in healthy ways, and seeking support when needed. It means setting healthy boundaries, practicing self-compassion, and engaging in activities that bring us joy and fulfillment. By nurturing our emotional well-being, we can build resilience, improve our relationships, and enhance our overall happiness.

Mental self-care focuses on nurturing our minds and intellectual growth. It involves engaging in activities that challenge and stimulate our brains, such as reading, learning new skills, or engaging in creative pursuits. Taking care of our mental well-being also means managing stress, practicing mindfulness and relaxation techniques, and seeking professional help when needed. By prioritizing mental self-care, we can enhance our cognitive abilities, improve our problem-solving skills, and cultivate a positive mindset.

Spiritual self-care is often overlooked but plays a significant role in our overall sense of fulfillment and purpose. It involves connecting with something greater than ourselves, whether through religious or spiritual practices, nature, or engaging in activities that align with our values and beliefs. By nurturing our spiritual well-being, we can find inner peace, gain clarity, and develop a deeper sense of meaning in our lives.

Recognizing and incorporating these different aspects of self-care into our daily lives is essential. Each aspect is interconnected and contributes to our overall well-being. By prioritizing self-care, we can prevent burnout, improve our relationships, and lead happier and more fulfilling lives.

Remember, self-care is not selfish; it is an act of self-love and self-preservation. So, take the time to recognize the different aspects of self-care and make them a priority in your life. Your well-being deserves your attention and nurturing. Start your journey towards self-care today and witness the transformative power it can have on your life.

The Neglect of Self-Care

In today's fast-paced and demanding world, it is all too easy to neglect our own well-being. We often find ourselves caught up in the never-ending cycle of work, family, and social obligations, leaving little time for self-care. However, the impotence of self-care cannot be overstated. It is a vital aspect of maintaining our physical, mental, and emotional health.

Self-care encompasses a wide range of activities that nourish and rejuvenate our mind, body, and soul. It involves prioritizing our own needs and taking deliberate steps to ensure our overall well-being. Unfortunately, many of us have become so accustomed to putting others first that we have forgotten how to take care of ourselves.

The neglect of self-care can have profound consequences on our health and happiness. Physically, it can lead to exhaustion, burnout, and a weakened immune system. Mentally and emotionally, it can result in increased stress, anxiety, and a sense of being overwhelmed.

By neglecting self-care, we rob ourselves of the opportunity to recharge and replenish our energy. We become depleted, unable to give our best to the people and activities that matter most to us. It is like trying to pour from an empty cup – eventually, we run dry.

To break free from the neglect of self-care, we must recognize its importance and make it a priority in our lives. This means setting boundaries, learning to say no when necessary, and carving out regular time for ourselves. It may involve activities such as exercise, meditation, spending time in nature, or simply indulging in a hobby we enjoy.

Remember, self-care is not a luxury; it is a necessity. It is not selfish; it is self-preserving. By taking care of ourselves, we become better equipped to care for others and fulfill our responsibilities more effectively.

In this subchapter, we will explore the reasons why self-care is often neglected and the detrimental effects it can have on our lives. We will delve into practical strategies and techniques to help us incorporate self-care into our daily routines. By prioritizing self-care, we can embark on a transformative journey towards nurturing ourselves and reclaiming our overall well-being.

Whether you are a busy professional, a stay-at-home parent, or anyone struggling to find balance amidst the chaos of life, this subchapter will provide you with the tools and insights you need to understand the impotence of self-care and take the necessary steps towards a more nurturing and fulfilling life. Remember, you deserve to be cared for, too.

Society's Influence on Neglecting Self-Care

In our fast-paced and demanding world, it is all too common for individuals to neglect their own self-care. Many factors contribute to this phenomenon, but one of the most significant influences is society itself. In this subchapter, we will explore how societal expectations, cultural norms, and the relentless pursuit of success can impede our ability to prioritize self-care.

Society bombards us with unrealistic ideals of perfection, perpetuating the belief that we must constantly strive to meet these unattainable standards. This relentless pursuit of perfection often leaves little room for self-care. We may find ourselves sacrificing our well-being, both physically and mentally, in the name of societal expectations. The pressure to excel in our careers, maintain a picture-perfect image, and juggle numerous responsibilities can leave us feeling overwhelmed and neglectful of our own needs.

Cultural norms also play a significant role in influencing our attitudes towards self-care. In some cultures, the concept of self-care is seen as indulgent or selfish, leading individuals to prioritize the needs of others before their own. This mindset creates a cycle of neglect, where individuals feel guilty for taking time to care for themselves. Additionally, cultural expectations regarding gender roles can further exacerbate the neglect of self-care. Men, in particular, may feel societal pressure to prioritize work and provide for their families, often at the expense of their own physical and mental well-being.

The impotence of self-care in society is also evident in the workplace. Many organizations prioritize productivity and output over the well-being of their employees. Long working hours, excessive workloads, and a lack of work-life balance can leave individuals feeling burnt out and incapable of prioritizing their own self-care. This perpetuates the belief that self-care is a luxury rather than a necessity.

To break free from society's influence on neglecting self-care, it is essential to recognize the importance of prioritizing our own well-being. Self-care is not selfish; it is a fundamental aspect of maintaining our physical, emotional, and mental health. By making a conscious effort to challenge societal norms and expectations, we can carve out time for self-care activities that nourish our mind, body, and soul.

In conclusion, society's influence on neglecting self-care is a significant barrier that hinders our ability to prioritize our well-being. We must acknowledge and challenge the unrealistic standards, cultural norms, and workplace pressures that contribute to this neglect. By doing so, we can embark on a journey towards self-care, reclaiming our health and happiness in a world that often overlooks its importance. Remember, self-care is not a luxury; it is a necessity for leading a fulfilling and balanced life.

Personal Factors Contributing to Neglecting Self-Care

In our fast-paced and demanding world, it is not uncommon for individuals to neglect their own self-care. The impotence of self-care is often overlooked, but it is crucial for maintaining our overall well-being. Understanding the personal factors that contribute to neglecting self-care can help us identify and address these issues, leading to a more balanced and fulfilling life.

One of the primary factors that contribute to neglecting self-care is a lack of awareness or knowledge about its importance. Many people are simply not aware of the detrimental effects that neglecting self-care can have on their physical, mental, and emotional health. They may be focused on meeting the needs of others or fulfilling their responsibilities, without realizing that taking care of themselves is equally important.

Another factor that contributes to neglecting self-care is the belief that it is selfish or indulgent. Society often promotes the idea that putting ourselves first is selfish, and we should always prioritize the needs of others. While it is indeed essential to be considerate and compassionate towards others, neglecting our own self-care can lead to burnout, stress, and a diminished ability to care for others effectively.

Additionally, personal factors such as perfectionism and high expectations can contribute to neglecting self-care. Many individuals feel the need to excel in their careers, be the perfect partner or parent, and maintain a flawless appearance. This relentless pursuit of perfection often leads to neglecting self-care, as individuals prioritize external achievements over their own well-being.

Furthermore, personal trauma or past experiences can also contribute to neglecting self-care. Individuals who have experienced abuse, neglect, or significant hardships may develop a belief that they do not deserve self-care or that prioritizing their own needs is not important. This can create a cycle of neglect that is challenging to break without proper support and guidance.

To overcome these personal factors contributing to neglecting self-care, it is crucial to prioritize self-awareness and self-compassion. Understanding the importance of self-care and recognizing that it is not selfish but necessary for our well-being is the first step. Setting realistic expectations, being kind to ourselves, and seeking support from loved ones or professionals can also help in breaking the cycle of neglect.

In conclusion, personal factors such as lack of awareness, societal beliefs, perfectionism, and past experiences can contribute to neglecting self-care. Recognizing and addressing these factors is essential for individuals to prioritize their own well-being and cultivate a healthy and balanced life. By understanding the impotence of self-care and taking proactive steps to nurture ourselves, we can lead happier, healthier, and more fulfilling lives.

Consequences of Neglecting Self-Care

In today's fast-paced and demanding world, many people tend to neglect the importance of self-care. Whether it is due to their busy schedules, societal expectations, or simply not prioritizing themselves, the consequences of neglecting self-care can be far-reaching and detrimental to one's overall well-being.

One of the most significant consequences of neglecting self-care is the decline in physical health. When we fail to take care of ourselves, our bodies suffer. We may experience increased stress levels, fatigue, weakened immune systems, and even develop chronic health conditions. Neglecting self-care can lead to poor eating habits, lack of exercise, and inadequate sleep, all of which can have long-term negative effects on our physical health.

Moreover, neglecting self-care can also impact our mental and emotional well-being. It is no secret that life can be challenging, and if we do not take the time to properly care for ourselves, our mental health may suffer. Neglecting self-care can contribute to increased anxiety, depression, and feelings of overwhelm. We may become more irritable, have difficulty concentrating, and experience a decreased ability to cope with daily stressors. Over time, this neglect can lead to burnout and a diminished sense of self-worth.

Another consequence of neglecting self-care is the strain it can place on our relationships. When we do not prioritize our own needs, it becomes challenging to show up fully for others. We may become more distant, less patient, and have difficulty maintaining meaningful connections. Neglecting self-care can also lead to resentment and frustration, as we may feel overwhelmed by the constant demands of others without taking time for ourselves.

Lastly, neglecting self-care can hinder personal growth and fulfillment. When we neglect our own needs and desires, we lose touch with our true selves. We may find ourselves stuck in unfulfilling routines, lacking passion and purpose in our lives. Neglecting self-care prevents us from exploring our interests, pursuing our dreams, and becoming the best version of ourselves.

In conclusion, neglecting self-care can have severe consequences on our physical, mental, and emotional well-being, as well as our relationships and personal growth. It is crucial for everyone to understand the impotence of self-care and prioritize it in their lives. By taking the time to care for ourselves, we can lead healthier, happier, and more fulfilling lives.

Physical Consequences

In our fast-paced and demanding world, we often forget the importance of taking care of ourselves. Neglecting our physical well-being can have severe consequences that affect every aspect of our lives. This subchapter aims to shed light on the physical consequences of neglecting self-care and emphasize the impotence of prioritizing our own well-being.

The human body is a remarkable machine that requires proper care and maintenance. When we fail to nurture ourselves, various physical consequences can arise. One of the most common consequences is chronic fatigue. Neglecting self-care leads to exhaustion, both physically and mentally, which can impact our ability to function effectively in our personal and professional lives. Lack of energy and constantly feeling drained can hinder our productivity and overall happiness.

Another physical consequence of neglecting self-care is weakened immune function. When we don't prioritize our health, our immune system becomes compromised, leaving us vulnerable to diseases and infections. Frequent illnesses, prolonged recovery periods, and a general feeling of being unwell become the norm. This weakened immune system can have long-term effects on our overall health and well-being.

Furthermore, neglecting self-care often leads to increased stress levels. Chronic stress can wreak havoc on our bodies, leading to a myriad of physical ailments such as headaches, muscle tension, digestive issues, and even cardiovascular problems. The mind-body connection is crucial, and neglecting one aspect can have a profound impact on the other.

Poor self-care habits also contribute to unhealthy lifestyle choices. When we neglect our physical well-being, we are more likely to engage in detrimental behaviors such as poor nutrition, lack of exercise, and inadequate sleep. These choices can lead to weight gain, increased risk of chronic illnesses, and a general decline in overall health.

Understanding the physical consequences of neglecting self-care is essential for everyone. It serves as a wake-up call, reminding us of the urgency to prioritize our own well-being. By taking the time to care for ourselves physically, we can improve our energy levels, boost our immune function, reduce stress, and make healthier lifestyle choices.

In conclusion, neglecting self-care has significant physical consequences that affect our overall health and well-being. By recognizing the impotence of self-care and making it a priority, we can avoid chronic fatigue, strengthen our immune system, reduce stress levels, and make healthier choices. Remember, self-care is not selfish; it is a necessary investment in our own physical and mental health.

Mental and Emotional Consequences

In our fast-paced and demanding world, it is easy to overlook the importance of self-care. We often prioritize our work, responsibilities, and the needs of others over our own mental and emotional well-being. However, neglecting ourselves can lead to severe consequences that affect every aspect of our lives.

One of the primary consequences of neglecting self-care is increased levels of stress and burnout. When we consistently put others' needs before our own, we deplete our mental and emotional reserves. This can lead to feelings of overwhelm, exhaustion, and a decreased ability to cope with everyday challenges. Moreover, chronic stress can contribute to the development of various physical and mental health issues, such as anxiety and depression.

Another consequence of neglecting self-care is a decline in overall mental health. Without taking the time to prioritize our own mental and emotional needs, we may find ourselves feeling disconnected, unhappy, and unfulfilled. Our mental health plays a crucial role in our ability to navigate life's ups and downs, build healthy relationships, and achieve personal goals. By neglecting self-care, we jeopardize our mental well-being and hinder our own growth and happiness.

Furthermore, neglecting self-care can lead to a negative impact on our relationships. When we are physically and emotionally drained, we may have less energy and patience to invest in our loved ones. This can result in strained relationships, conflicts, and feelings of resentment. Additionally, our ability to communicate effectively and empathize with others may be compromised when we neglect our own mental and emotional needs.

The consequences of neglecting self-care are not limited to our personal lives; they also spill over into our professional lives. Impotence in self-care can lead to decreased productivity, poor decision-making, and an overall lack of motivation. When we neglect ourselves, we are more prone to experiencing job dissatisfaction, increased absenteeism, and a higher risk of professional burnout.

Recognizing the mental and emotional consequences of neglecting self-care is the first step towards change. By prioritizing our mental and emotional well-being, we can cultivate resilience, build healthier relationships, and enhance our overall quality of life. It is crucial to carve out time for self-care activities that rejuvenate our minds, nourish our souls, and replenish our emotional reserves. Remember, self-care is not selfish; it is a vital investment in our own happiness and well-being.

Social and Relationship Consequences

In our fast-paced and demanding world, the importance of self-care cannot be overstated. Neglecting our own well-being can have severe consequences, not only for our physical and mental health but also for our social and relationship dynamics. This subchapter will explore the profound impact that neglecting self-care can have on our social interactions and personal connections.

One of the most evident social consequences of neglecting self-care is the strain it puts on our relationships. When we are constantly running on empty, feeling exhausted and overwhelmed, it becomes challenging to truly connect with others. Our emotional reserves are depleted, making it difficult to engage in meaningful conversations, empathize with loved ones, and be fully present in their lives. As a result, relationships can suffer, leading to feelings of isolation, detachment, and even resentment.

Furthermore, neglecting self-care can also erode our ability to set boundaries and communicate effectively. Without taking the time to nurture ourselves, we may find it challenging to express our needs and desires clearly. This can create misunderstandings, conflict, and a sense of being taken advantage of in our relationships. Over time, this can lead to a breakdown in trust and intimacy, making it even more difficult to foster healthy connections with others.

Another social consequence of neglecting self-care is the impact it has on our social support networks. When we fail to prioritize our own well-being, we may inadvertently distance ourselves from the people who could provide us with the support and encouragement we need.

By neglecting self-care, we may become less engaged in social activities, withdraw from social gatherings, and isolate ourselves. This isolation can leave us feeling unsupported and disconnected from those around us, ultimately exacerbating feelings of loneliness and exacerbating our overall well-being.

Recognizing the social and relationship consequences of neglecting self-care is crucial for everyone. It is not only about taking care of ourselves but also about nurturing our connections with others. By prioritizing self-care, we can cultivate the emotional resilience and energy needed to engage meaningfully with our loved ones. We can set healthy boundaries and communicate our needs effectively, fostering trust and intimacy. Moreover, by taking care of ourselves, we can build a strong social support network, ensuring we have the love and encouragement we need during challenging times.

Remember, self-care is not a selfish act; it is an essential component of a healthy and fulfilling life. By investing in our own well-being, we can create a positive ripple effect that extends to all areas of our lives, including our relationships. So, let us embark on this journey towards self-care, nurturing ourselves and our connections with others along the way.

Chapter 2: Exploring the Journey

Acknowledging the Need for Self-Care

In our fast-paced and demanding world, it is easy to get caught up in the whirlwind of responsibilities and forget about taking care of ourselves. The impotence of self-care cannot be overstated, as neglecting our own well-being can have serious consequences for our physical, mental, and emotional health. In this subchapter, we will explore the importance of acknowledging the need for self-care and how it can transform our lives.

For far too long, self-care has been viewed as a luxury or an indulgence, something we only deserve when we have completed all our tasks and responsibilities. However, this mindset is flawed and often leads to burnout, exhaustion, and a general sense of dissatisfaction with life. It is crucial to recognize that self-care is not selfish; it is an essential practice that allows us to recharge, rejuvenate, and show up fully in all aspects of our lives.

One of the main reasons why self-care is so crucial is its impact on our physical health. Neglecting our bodies can result in increased stress levels, weakened immune systems, and a higher risk of developing chronic illnesses. By acknowledging the need for self-care, we can prioritize activities that nourish our bodies, such as regular exercise, nutritious meals, and sufficient sleep. These simple yet powerful practices can significantly improve our overall well-being and prevent future health complications.

Furthermore, self-care plays a vital role in our mental and emotional well-being. In a world that often feels overwhelming and chaotic, taking time for ourselves allows us to find inner peace and balance. Engaging in activities we enjoy, such as reading, meditating, or pursuing hobbies, can reduce stress, enhance our mood, and boost our creativity. It is through self-care that we can cultivate self-love, acceptance, and a deeper understanding of our own needs and desires.

To truly acknowledge the need for self-care, we must overcome the societal conditioning that tells us we must always put others first. While caring for others is admirable, it should not come at the expense of our own well-being. By prioritizing self-care, we can become better partners, friends, parents, and professionals. We can show up with more compassion, empathy, and energy, ready to support and uplift those around us.

In conclusion, self-care is not a luxury; it is a necessity. By acknowledging the need for self-care, we can transform our lives and create a healthier, more fulfilling existence. It is time to break free from the belief that self-care is selfish and embrace the fact that it is an essential practice for our physical, mental, and emotional well-being. Let us embark on this journey towards self-care together, nurturing ourselves and others along the way.

Recognizing the Signs of Neglecting Self-Care

In today's fast-paced and demanding world, it is all too easy to neglect our own well-being in the pursuit of success, productivity, and taking care of others. However, failing to prioritize self-care can lead to a range of negative consequences, both physically and mentally. It is essential for everyone to recognize the signs of neglecting self-care in order to prevent burnout and maintain a healthy, balanced lifestyle.

One of the most common signs of neglecting self-care is chronic fatigue. Constantly feeling tired, lacking energy, and struggling to focus on daily tasks can indicate that you are not giving yourself the rest and rejuvenation you need. Additionally, neglecting self-care often goes hand in hand with neglecting proper nutrition. Poor eating habits, such as skipping meals or relying on processed foods, can lead to a weakened immune system, weight gain or loss, and an overall decline in physical health.

Another sign of neglecting self-care is increased stress and anxiety. When you consistently put others' needs above your own and fail to set boundaries, it can result in heightened levels of stress and emotional exhaustion. This can manifest in feelings of irritability, frequent mood swings, and an inability to cope with everyday challenges. Neglected self-care can also lead to a decline in mental health, including symptoms of depression, loneliness, and a decreased sense of self-worth.

Recognizing the signs of neglecting self-care is crucial because it allows you to take proactive steps towards addressing the issue and prioritizing your well-being. It is important to remember that self-care is not selfish, but rather a necessary act of self-preservation. By taking the time to engage in activities that bring you joy, practicing mindfulness, and setting aside dedicated time for rest and relaxation, you can effectively combat the negative effects of neglecting self-care.

In conclusion, neglecting self-care can have serious consequences on both our physical and mental well-being. It is essential for everyone to be aware of the signs of neglecting self-care in order to prevent burnout and maintain a healthy, balanced lifestyle. By recognizing the signs such as chronic fatigue, increased stress, and declining mental health, we can take the necessary steps to prioritize self-care and nurture ourselves. Remember, self-care is not a luxury but a vital component of leading a fulfilling and happy life.

Understanding the Importance of Prioritizing Self-Care

In our fast-paced and demanding world, it is easy to get caught up in the busyness of life and neglect our own well-being. However, the importance of prioritizing self-care cannot be overstated. Taking care of ourselves physically, mentally, and emotionally is essential for leading a fulfilling and balanced life.

Self-care is not a luxury; it is a necessity. It involves making choices that promote our overall well-being and happiness. Many individuals tend to put others' needs before their own, but neglecting ourselves can lead to burnout, stress, and even physical and mental health issues. By prioritizing self-care, we are better equipped to handle life's challenges and take care of others effectively.

One of the key reasons why self-care is important is that it helps us maintain our physical health. Engaging in regular exercise, eating nutritious meals, and getting enough sleep are all crucial aspects of self-care. When we prioritize our physical well-being, we have more energy, feel more alert, and are better equipped to cope with daily demands.

Self-care also plays a significant role in our mental and emotional well-being. Taking time for activities we enjoy, such as hobbies or spending time with loved ones, helps reduce stress and improve our overall mood. Engaging in self-reflection and practicing mindfulness can help us manage our emotions and cultivate a positive mindset.

Additionally, self-care enables us to set boundaries and prioritize our own needs. By recognizing and honoring our limits, we avoid becoming overwhelmed and ensure that we are giving ourselves the care we deserve. This can lead to increased self-esteem and a greater sense of self-worth.

It is important to note that self-care looks different for everyone. It is a personal journey that requires self-awareness and experimentation. What works for one person may not work for another. It is about finding activities and practices that nourish and rejuvenate us individually.

In conclusion, understanding the importance of prioritizing self-care is crucial for everyone. By making self-care a priority, we invest in our physical, mental, and emotional well-being, which ultimately leads to a happier and more fulfilling life. Remember, self-care is not selfish; it is an act of self-love and self-preservation. Take the time to nurture yourself and make self-care a non-negotiable part of your daily routine.

Overcoming Barriers to Self-Care

Self-care is crucial for leading a healthy and fulfilling life, yet many individuals struggle to prioritize it. In our fast-paced and demanding world, it is easy to neglect our own needs and well-being. However, it is important to recognize the barriers that prevent us from engaging in self-care and find ways to overcome them.

One of the main barriers to self-care is the belief that it is selfish or indulgent. Many individuals, especially those who are caregivers or have demanding jobs, feel guilty for taking time for themselves. However, self-care is not selfish; it is essential for our mental, emotional, and physical well-being. By prioritizing self-care, we can better serve others and be more present in our roles.

Another barrier is the lack of time. Our schedules are often filled with commitments, leaving little room for self-care activities. However, it is important to remember that self-care does not have to be time-consuming. It can be as simple as taking a few minutes each day to practice deep breathing, engaging in a hobby, or going for a short walk. By making small adjustments to our routines, we can carve out time for self-care.

A common barrier that many face is the fear of judgment and criticism. Society often glorifies busyness and productivity, making self-care seem like a luxury rather than a necessity. However, it is essential to prioritize our own needs and set boundaries. Remember that your well-being is important, and taking care of yourself is not something to be ashamed of.

Financial constraints can also be a barrier to self-care. Many self-care activities such as spa treatments or vacations can be expensive. However, self-care does not have to be costly. There are plenty of free or low-cost activities that can be just as rejuvenating, such as reading a book, taking a bath, or practicing mindfulness.

To overcome these barriers, it is important to shift our mindset and prioritize self-care as a non-negotiable part of our lives. Start by recognizing the importance of self-care and the positive impact it can have on your overall well-being. Set realistic goals and make a commitment to yourself. Seek support from loved ones or join a community of like-minded individuals who can provide encouragement and accountability.

Remember, self-care is not a luxury, but a necessity. By overcoming these barriers and embracing self-care, you can lead a more balanced, joyful, and fulfilling life. Take the first step towards a journey of self-care and transform neglect into nurturing.

Identifying Internal Barriers

In the pursuit of self-care, it is crucial to recognize and address the internal barriers that may hinder our ability to prioritize our well-being. These barriers can manifest in various forms and may differ from person to person. However, understanding and acknowledging these obstacles is an essential step towards nurturing ourselves and leading a fulfilling life.

One common internal barrier is the belief that self-care is a luxury rather than a necessity. Many individuals find themselves trapped in a cycle of neglecting their needs, convincing themselves that they do not have the time or resources to prioritize self-care. This mindset often stems from societal expectations and the pressure to constantly be productive. However, it is essential to realize that self-care is not selfish; it is an act of self-preservation that allows us to better serve others and lead more balanced lives.

Another internal barrier is the fear of judgment or guilt associated with taking time for oneself. Society often glorifies busyness and self-sacrifice, making it challenging for individuals to prioritize their own well-being without feeling guilty. It is crucial to recognize that self-care is not a selfish act, but rather an act of self-love and self-respect. By taking care of ourselves, we become better equipped to care for others.

Additionally, negative self-talk and low self-esteem can serve as significant barriers to practicing self-care. If we do not believe that we deserve care and attention, it becomes difficult to prioritize our well-being. It is essential to challenge these negative beliefs and replace them with positive affirmations that reinforce our self-worth and the importance of self-care.

Identifying these internal barriers is the first step towards overcoming them. By acknowledging and understanding the obstacles that prevent us from prioritizing self-care, we can develop strategies to overcome them. This may involve setting boundaries, learning to say no, seeking support from loved ones, or incorporating small acts of self-care into our daily routines.

Remember, self-care is not a luxury; it is a fundamental aspect of our overall well-being. By identifying and addressing the internal barriers that impede our ability to practice self-care, we can embark on a journey towards nurturing ourselves and leading more fulfilling lives. It is time to break free from the cycle of neglect and prioritize our well-being, one small step at a time.

To all those who feel the impotence of self-care, it is time to reclaim your power and prioritize your well-being. You are worthy of love, care, and attention. Start by identifying the internal barriers that hold you back, challenge negative beliefs, and make a commitment to yourself. Remember, self-care is not a destination; it is a continuous journey towards nurturing your body, mind, and soul.

Addressing External Barriers

In our journey towards self-care, it is crucial to understand that there are external barriers that can hinder our progress. These barriers often go unnoticed, but they play a significant role in preventing us from nurturing ourselves. It is essential to identify and address these barriers so that we can overcome them and prioritize our well-being.

One of the most common external barriers to self-care is the lack of time. In today's fast-paced world, we are constantly bombarded with commitments and responsibilities. Our schedules become overloaded, leaving little or no time for ourselves. However, it is vital to recognize that self-care is not a luxury but a necessity. By making small adjustments to our daily routines and carving out dedicated time for self-care activities, we can gradually overcome this barrier and put ourselves first.

Another external barrier is societal pressure and expectations. Often, we find ourselves caught up in meeting the expectations of others, whether it be at work, in our relationships, or within our communities. This pressure can lead to neglecting our own needs and well-being. Addressing this barrier requires setting healthy boundaries and learning to prioritize ourselves without feeling guilty. It is essential to understand that taking care of ourselves enables us to show up better for others.

Financial constraints can also act as external barriers to self-care. Many people believe that self-care requires expensive spa treatments or luxurious vacations. However, self-care can be simple and affordable. It can involve activities such as taking a walk in nature, practicing mindfulness, or engaging in creative hobbies. By exploring low-cost or free self-care options, we can overcome the financial barrier and make self-care accessible to everyone.

Finally, a lack of support or understanding from family, friends, or colleagues can hinder our self-care efforts. It is crucial to surround ourselves with a supportive network of individuals who understand and respect our need for self-care. By communicating our needs and boundaries to those around us, we can create an environment that fosters self-care and encourages others to prioritize their well-being as well.

Addressing these external barriers may require time, effort, and persistence. However, by acknowledging their existence and actively working to overcome them, we can create a nurturing environment for ourselves. Remember, self-care is not selfish; it is an essential aspect of maintaining our overall well-being. By prioritizing ourselves and addressing external barriers, we can embark on a journey towards self-care that will positively impact every aspect of our lives.

Building a Foundation for Self-Care

In today's fast-paced and demanding world, it is easy to neglect our own well-being and prioritize the needs of others ahead of our own. However, understanding the importance of self-care is vital for leading a fulfilling and balanced life. In this subchapter, we will explore how to build a strong foundation for self-care and its implications on our overall well-being.

Self-care is not a luxury; it is a necessity. It is about taking deliberate actions to nurture and nourish ourselves physically, mentally, and emotionally. Neglecting self-care can lead to a myriad of negative consequences, such as burnout, increased stress levels, and a diminished sense of self-worth. Recognizing the impotence of self-care is the first step towards a transformative journey of self-discovery and personal growth.

Building a foundation for self-care begins with self-awareness. Take the time to reflect on your needs, desires, and values. Understand what truly brings you joy and fulfillment. This self-reflection will help you prioritize self-care activities that align with your personal goals and aspirations.

Next, establish healthy boundaries. Learn to say no when necessary and set realistic expectations for yourself. Boundaries are essential for protecting your physical and emotional well-being. By setting clear boundaries, you can create space for self-care without feeling guilty or overwhelmed.

Another crucial aspect of building a foundation for self-care is developing a self-care routine. This routine should encompass activities that nourish your mind, body, and soul. Consider incorporating activities such as exercise, meditation, journaling, or engaging in hobbies that bring you happiness. By scheduling regular self-care activities, you are prioritizing your well-being and ensuring that you make time for yourself amidst the chaos of daily life.

Furthermore, seek support from loved ones or professionals. Surround yourself with individuals who understand and encourage your journey towards self-care. A strong support system can provide guidance, accountability, and a sense of belonging, making the path towards self-care more enjoyable and sustainable.

Remember, self-care is a lifelong journey, not a destination. It requires consistent effort and a commitment to yourself. Building a foundation for self-care is about finding balance, setting boundaries, and actively prioritizing your well-being. By investing in self-care, you are investing in your overall happiness, success, and fulfillment. So, embark on this transformative journey and witness the positive impact it can have on every aspect of your life.

Setting Personal Boundaries

In the fast-paced and demanding world we live in, self-care has become increasingly crucial for our overall well-being. Taking care of ourselves is not only a luxury but a necessity, as neglecting our own needs can lead to burnout, stress, and a diminished sense of self-worth. One vital aspect of self-care that often goes unnoticed is setting personal boundaries.

Personal boundaries act as a protective shield, safeguarding our physical, emotional, and mental well-being. They define the limits of what is acceptable and unacceptable in our interactions with others. Without clear boundaries, we are vulnerable to being taken advantage of, overwhelmed, and drained of our energy.

Setting personal boundaries can be challenging, especially for those who have always put others' needs before their own. However, learning to establish and maintain healthy boundaries is a powerful step towards reclaiming control over our lives and fostering self-empowerment.

First and foremost, it is essential to recognize that setting boundaries is not selfish or inconsiderate. It is an act of self-love and self-respect, asserting that our needs and feelings are just as valid as anyone else's. By setting boundaries, we communicate our limits and expectations to others, ensuring that our well-being remains a priority.

To begin setting personal boundaries, it is crucial to identify our values, needs, and limits. Reflect on what is truly important to you and what you need to feel happy, fulfilled, and safe. This self-reflection will help you determine what boundaries are necessary to establish in different areas of your life, such as relationships, work, and leisure.

Once you have identified your boundaries, it is important to communicate them assertively and confidently. Clearly express your limits and expectations to others, using "I" statements and focusing on your feelings rather than blaming or criticizing. Remember that setting boundaries is not about controlling or changing others; it is about taking responsibility for our own well-being.

Setting personal boundaries may require practice and consistency. It is natural to encounter resistance or pushback from others who may be accustomed to crossing our boundaries. However, stay firm and committed to your own self-care. Surround yourself with supportive individuals who respect and encourage your boundaries.

In conclusion, setting personal boundaries is a vital aspect of self-care. It enables us to protect our well-being, maintain healthy relationships, and cultivate a sense of self-worth. By recognizing the importance of personal boundaries and actively implementing them in our lives, we embark on a transformative journey towards self-nurturing and empowerment. Remember, you deserve to set the boundaries that will allow you to flourish and thrive.

Establishing Healthy Habits and Routines

In today's fast-paced world, many of us find ourselves neglecting our own well-being in pursuit of our goals and responsibilities. We often prioritize work, family, and other obligations over taking care of ourselves. However, it is crucial to understand the importance of self-care and the impact it can have on our overall health and happiness.

This subchapter, titled "Establishing Healthy Habits and Routines," aims to guide you on a transformative journey towards self-care. Whether you have been neglecting your own needs for far too long or simply wish to enhance your existing self-care practices, this chapter is designed to provide you with valuable insights and practical tips.

First and foremost, it is vital to recognize the impotence of self-care. Many individuals mistakenly believe that focusing on their own well-being is selfish or indulgent. However, self-care is not a luxury; it is a necessity. By neglecting self-care, we risk burnout, diminished mental health, and even physical ailments. Therefore, this chapter encourages you to shift your mindset and understand that taking care of yourself is essential to being able to care for others effectively.

One of the key aspects of establishing healthy habits and routines is self-awareness. Understanding your own needs, desires, and limits is crucial in designing a self-care practice that suits you. This chapter will provide you with tools and exercises to enhance self-awareness and help you identify areas in your life that require attention.

Additionally, you will learn the importance of setting boundaries and saying no. Many individuals struggle with prioritizing their own needs because they fear disappointing others. However, by setting healthy boundaries and learning to say no when necessary, you can create a space for self-care without guilt or resentment.

Furthermore, this chapter will explore various self-care practices and rituals that you can incorporate into your daily life. From mindfulness exercises and relaxation techniques to physical activities and healthy eating habits, you will discover a wide range of options to suit your preferences and needs.

In conclusion, establishing healthy habits and routines is a fundamental step towards nurturing yourself and embracing self-care. By recognizing the impotence of self-care, practicing self-awareness, setting boundaries, and incorporating various self-care practices into your life, you can embark on a transformative journey towards overall well-being and happiness. Remember, self-care is not a luxury, but a necessity, and it is never too late to prioritize yourself and discover the immense benefits it can bring to your life.

Chapter 3: Self-Care Practices

Physical Self-Care

In today's fast-paced and demanding world, self-care has become more important than ever. Taking care of our physical well-being is a fundamental aspect of self-care that often gets neglected. This subchapter aims to shed light on the importance of physical self-care and provide practical tips to incorporate it into our daily lives.

Physical self-care encompasses all activities that contribute to our overall physical health and well-being. It involves nourishing our bodies through proper nutrition, engaging in regular exercise, prioritizing sleep, and managing stress. Neglecting our physical self-care can lead to various health issues, decreased energy levels, and a diminished quality of life.

One of the primary reasons for the impotence of self-care is the misconception that it is a selfish act. However, this couldn't be further from the truth. When we take care of ourselves physically, we are better equipped to take care of others and fulfill our responsibilities. It's like the oxygen mask analogy on an airplane – we need to secure our own mask first before helping others.

To prioritize physical self-care, start by examining your daily routine. Are you getting enough sleep? Are you making healthy food choices? Are you incorporating exercise into your daily routine? If not, it's time to make some changes.

Begin by setting aside dedicated time for sleep. Aim for a consistent sleep schedule, ensuring you get the recommended 7-8 hours of quality sleep each night. Create a relaxing bedtime routine, such as reading a book or taking a warm bath, to signal to your body that it's time to wind down.

Next, pay attention to your diet. Incorporate a variety of fruits, vegetables, whole grains, and lean proteins into your meals. Stay hydrated by drinking plenty of water throughout the day. Limit your intake of processed foods, sugary drinks, and alcohol.

Regular exercise is another crucial aspect of physical self-care. Find activities that you enjoy and make them a part of your routine. It could be walking, jogging, yoga, dancing, or any other form of movement that gets your body moving and your heart rate up. Exercise not only helps to maintain a healthy weight but also boosts mood, reduces stress, and improves overall well-being.

Lastly, manage stress effectively. Stress can take a toll on our physical health, so it's essential to find healthy coping mechanisms. Engage in activities that help you relax and unwind, such as meditation, deep breathing exercises, or engaging in hobbies you enjoy.

Remember, physical self-care is not a luxury, but a necessity. By prioritizing our physical well-being, we can lead healthier, more fulfilling lives. Embrace the impotence of self-care and take the necessary steps towards nurturing your physical self today.

Nurturing Your Body Through Exercise

Exercise plays a vital role in nurturing your body and is an essential component of self-care. In our fast-paced and hectic lives, we often neglect the importance of taking care of ourselves. However, understanding the impotence of self-care can lead us on a journey towards a healthier and happier life.

Regular exercise offers numerous benefits to both our physical and mental well-being. It not only helps us maintain a healthy weight but also improves cardiovascular health, strengthens our muscles and bones, and reduces the risk of chronic diseases such as diabetes and heart disease. Additionally, exercise releases endorphins, the feel-good hormones, which can enhance our mood, reduce stress, and alleviate symptoms of anxiety and depression.

Regardless of age, gender, or fitness level, everyone can benefit from incorporating exercise into their daily routine. The key is finding activities that you enjoy and that align with your personal preferences and physical abilities. Whether it's going for a brisk walk, dancing, swimming, or joining a fitness class, there are countless options to choose from. The important thing is to prioritize and make time for exercise regularly.

It's important to start slow and gradually increase the intensity and duration of your workouts to avoid injuries. Remember, exercising shouldn't be a punishment but rather a way to nourish and take care of your body. Set realistic goals and celebrate your achievements along the way to stay motivated.

Incorporating exercise into your daily routine doesn't have to be a burden. You can make it enjoyable by involving friends or family members, listening to music or podcasts while working out, or exploring nature during outdoor activities. The key is to find what works best for you and make it a sustainable part of your lifestyle.

If you're struggling with motivation, try to focus on the positive outcomes of exercise. Think about how good you will feel after a workout, the stress relief it provides, and the long-term health benefits you'll gain. Remember, self-care is not selfish; it's essential for your overall well-being.

In conclusion, nurturing your body through exercise is an integral part of self-care. It promotes physical fitness, mental well-being, and reduces the risk of chronic diseases. No matter your current fitness level, there are exercise options available for everyone. By prioritizing regular exercise and making it an enjoyable part of your routine, you can embark on a journey towards a healthier and happier life. Remember, taking care of yourself is not a luxury but a necessity.

Prioritizing Nutrition for Optimal Well-Being

In our fast-paced modern world, it is easy to neglect our own well-being. We often find ourselves caught up in the demands of work, family, and countless other responsibilities. However, taking care of ourselves is crucial for our overall health and happiness. One key aspect of self-care that is often overlooked is nutrition.

Nutrition plays a vital role in our well-being, affecting our physical and mental health in numerous ways. The food we consume serves as fuel for our bodies, providing the necessary nutrients for optimal functioning. A balanced diet rich in vitamins, minerals, and other essential components helps strengthen our immune system, increases energy levels, and improves cognitive function.

When it comes to self-care, prioritizing nutrition means making conscious choices about the food we eat. It means opting for whole, unprocessed foods instead of relying on convenience or fast food options. It means incorporating a variety of fruits, vegetables, lean proteins, whole grains, and healthy fats into our diets.

By prioritizing nutrition, we can reduce the risk of chronic diseases such as heart disease, diabetes, and obesity. A diet high in fruits and vegetables, for example, has been linked to a lower risk of heart disease and certain types of cancer. Additionally, proper nutrition can help manage weight, improve digestion, and promote better sleep patterns.

Aside from the physical benefits, nutrition also plays a crucial role in our mental well-being. Studies have shown that certain nutrients can positively impact our mood, cognition, and overall mental health. Omega-3 fatty acids, found in fatty fish like salmon, have been linked to a reduced risk of depression and anxiety. Similarly, foods rich in B vitamins, such as whole grains and leafy greens, can support brain health and improve cognitive function.

In conclusion, prioritizing nutrition is a fundamental aspect of self-care. By making conscious choices about the food we consume, we can significantly improve our overall well-being. A healthy, balanced diet provides the necessary nutrients for optimal physical and mental health, reducing the risk of chronic diseases and promoting a better quality of life. Remember, taking care of ourselves is not a luxury but a necessity. Start prioritizing your nutrition today and embark on a journey towards self-care and optimal well-being.

Emotional Self-Care

In our fast-paced and demanding world, it is all too easy to neglect our own emotional well-being. We often prioritize the needs of others over our own, leaving us feeling depleted and emotionally drained. However, recognizing the importance of self-care and taking proactive steps to nurture our emotional health is essential for leading a fulfilling and balanced life.

Emotional self-care refers to the practice of actively tending to our emotional needs and engaging in activities that promote emotional well-being. It involves acknowledging and accepting our emotions, prioritizing self-compassion, and developing healthy coping mechanisms to navigate life's challenges.

One of the fundamental aspects of emotional self-care is self-awareness. It is crucial to take the time to check in with ourselves regularly, allowing us to identify and understand our emotions. By recognizing our feelings, we can better address them and prevent them from becoming overwhelming or manifesting as physical symptoms. Journaling, meditation, or simply taking a few moments of solitude can help us cultivate this self-awareness.

Another essential aspect of emotional self-care is self-compassion. Often, we are our own harshest critics, feeding into negative self-talk and self-judgment. Practicing self-compassion involves treating ourselves with kindness, understanding, and forgiveness. We must learn to embrace our imperfections and be gentle with ourselves during times of struggle or failure. Engaging in activities that bring us joy and remind us of our worth can significantly contribute to building self-compassion.

Developing healthy coping mechanisms is equally vital for emotional self-care. Life throws curveballs at us all the time, and it is crucial to have strategies in place to navigate through difficult emotions. This may involve seeking support from loved ones, engaging in therapeutic activities such as art or music, or even seeking professional help when needed. By actively finding healthy ways to cope with stress, sadness, or anxiety, we can prevent these emotions from overwhelming us and maintain a sense of balance.

Emotional self-care is not a luxury but a necessity. By prioritizing our emotional well-being, we equip ourselves with the tools to navigate life's challenges effectively and find greater fulfillment. Remember that you deserve to feel emotionally nurtured and cared for. Take the time to understand your emotions, practice self-compassion, and develop healthy coping mechanisms. Your emotional well-being matters, and by investing in it, you are investing in a happier and more contented life.

Practicing Mindfulness and Meditation

In our fast-paced, chaotic world, self-care has become an imperative for everyone. Neglecting our own well-being can lead to burnout, anxiety, and a general sense of dissatisfaction with life. One powerful tool that can help us navigate these challenges is the practice of mindfulness and meditation.

Mindfulness is the practice of bringing our attention to the present moment, without judgment. It involves being fully aware of our thoughts, emotions, and sensations as they arise, and learning to observe them without getting caught up in them. By cultivating mindfulness, we can develop a greater sense of self-awareness and gain control over our reactions to stressful situations.

Meditation, on the other hand, is a specific technique that allows us to train our minds and cultivate a state of calm and clarity. By practicing meditation regularly, we can improve our ability to focus, reduce stress, and enhance our overall well-being. It provides a space for self-reflection and introspection, allowing us to connect with our inner selves and cultivate a sense of peace and tranquility.

The importance of incorporating mindfulness and meditation into our self-care routine cannot be understated. These practices have been scientifically proven to have numerous benefits, both for our physical and mental health. Regular mindfulness and meditation practice can reduce anxiety and depression, lower blood pressure, improve sleep quality, and boost our immune system.

Moreover, mindfulness and meditation help us cultivate a deeper sense of self-compassion and acceptance. By learning to be present with our thoughts and emotions, we can develop a kinder and more understanding attitude towards ourselves. This self-compassion, in turn, enables us to nurture and care for ourselves in a more meaningful way.

To begin incorporating mindfulness and meditation into your self-care routine, start by setting aside a few minutes each day to sit quietly and focus on your breath. You can also explore guided meditation apps or attend meditation classes to deepen your practice. Remember, consistency is key. Even just a few minutes of daily practice can yield significant results over time.

In conclusion, practicing mindfulness and meditation is an essential component of self-care. By developing the skills of mindfulness and engaging in regular meditation, we can improve our overall well-being, reduce stress, and cultivate a greater sense of self-compassion. So, take a moment each day to pause, breathe, and connect with your inner self. Your journey towards self-care begins now.

Engaging in Creative Outlets for Emotional Expression

In our fast-paced and often demanding world, it's easy to neglect our emotional well-being. From balancing work and personal responsibilities to dealing with daily stressors, we often forget the importance of self-care. However, taking the time to engage in creative outlets for emotional expression can have a profound impact on our overall well-being.

Creative outlets provide a unique and powerful way to express our emotions. Whether it's through painting, writing, dancing, or playing an instrument, these activities allow us to tap into our innermost thoughts and feelings. Engaging in these outlets can be cathartic, allowing us to release pent-up emotions and gain a deeper understanding of ourselves.

One of the key benefits of creative outlets for emotional expression is their ability to provide a sense of release and relief. When we engage in these activities, we allow ourselves to let go of the stress and tension we may be holding onto. This release can be incredibly freeing, allowing us to experience a sense of lightness and clarity.

Furthermore, creative outlets can also serve as a form of self-discovery. By engaging in activities that allow us to express ourselves creatively, we gain new insights into our own emotions, desires, and fears. This self-awareness is crucial for personal growth and can help us navigate through life's challenges with greater resilience and understanding.

Moreover, creative outlets provide a safe space for emotional expression. In a society that often discourages vulnerability, engaging in creative activities allows us to let our guard down and explore our emotions without judgment. This safe space fosters self-acceptance and self-compassion, allowing us to embrace our emotions fully.

It's important to note that there is no right or wrong way to engage in creative outlets for emotional expression. The goal is not to create a masterpiece but rather to use these activities as a means of connecting with ourselves on a deeper level. The process itself is what matters, not the end result.

In conclusion, engaging in creative outlets for emotional expression is an essential aspect of self-care. It allows us to release pent-up emotions, gain self-awareness, and create a safe space for emotional exploration. Regardless of our individual circumstances, finding time for these activities can greatly enhance our overall well-being. So, let us all nurture our emotional selves by embracing the power of creative outlets.

Mental Self-Care

In today's fast-paced and demanding world, taking care of our mental well-being is of utmost importance. Neglecting our mental health can lead to a range of negative consequences, including increased stress, anxiety, and even depression. This subchapter aims to shed light on the importance of mental self-care and how it can positively impact our overall well-being.

Self-care is often associated with physical wellness, such as eating a balanced diet and engaging in regular exercise. However, mental self-care is equally vital for maintaining a healthy and fulfilling life. It involves practices and activities that promote mental resilience, emotional well-being, and inner peace.

One of the key aspects of mental self-care is managing stress. Stress can have a detrimental effect on our mental health, leading to burnout and a loss of motivation. By incorporating stress management techniques into our daily routines, such as mindfulness meditation, deep breathing exercises, or engaging in hobbies we enjoy, we can effectively reduce stress levels and improve our mental state.

Additionally, self-care involves nurturing positive relationships and setting healthy boundaries. Surrounding ourselves with supportive and understanding individuals can significantly impact our mental well-being. Regularly connecting with loved ones, seeking social support, and sharing our thoughts and feelings can foster a sense of belonging and emotional support.

Practicing self-compassion is another crucial aspect of mental self-care. Many individuals tend to be overly critical of themselves, leading to feelings of inadequacy and low self-esteem. By practicing self-compassion, we can learn to treat ourselves with kindness and understanding, embracing our imperfections and celebrating our accomplishments.

Engaging in activities that bring us joy and fulfillment is also essential for mental self-care. Whether it's pursuing a hobby, spending time in nature, or engaging in creative outlets, these activities provide a much-needed break from the daily stresses of life and can rejuvenate our mental state.

In conclusion, mental self-care is of utmost importance for individuals of all walks of life. Neglecting our mental well-being can have serious consequences on our overall health and happiness. By incorporating stress management techniques, nurturing positive relationships, practicing self-compassion, and engaging in activities that bring us joy, we can cultivate a healthy and resilient mind. Remember, taking care of your mental health is not selfish; it is an investment in your overall well-being and the key to leading a fulfilling and balanced life.

Cultivating a Positive Mindset

In the journey towards self-care, one of the most significant aspects is cultivating a positive mindset. A positive mindset is the foundation upon which self-care thrives, as it shapes our thoughts, emotions, and actions towards a healthier and more fulfilling life. This subchapter aims to explore the importance of cultivating a positive mindset and provide practical tips on how to do so.

For everyone, regardless of their background or circumstances, self-care is crucial. It is the act of intentionally taking care of ourselves physically, mentally, and emotionally. However, many individuals neglect this aspect of their lives, often due to the demands of work, relationships, or societal pressures. This neglect can lead to increased stress, burnout, and overall dissatisfaction with life.

One key factor in self-care is cultivating a positive mindset. It is about adopting a perspective that focuses on the positive aspects of life, even in the face of challenges. A positive mindset enables individuals to approach difficulties with resilience, optimism, and hope. It allows them to reframe negative situations, learn from them, and grow stronger as a result.

To cultivate a positive mindset, it is essential to practice self-awareness. This involves being mindful of our thoughts and emotions, recognizing negative patterns, and consciously choosing to shift towards positivity. It also involves surrounding ourselves with positive influences, such as supportive friends, uplifting books or podcasts, and engaging in activities that bring us joy and fulfillment.

Another effective way to cultivate a positive mindset is through daily affirmations and gratitude practices. Affirmations are positive statements that we repeat to ourselves to reinforce positive beliefs and attitudes. Gratitude practices involve acknowledging and appreciating the things we are grateful for in our lives. By incorporating these practices into our daily routines, we train our minds to focus on the good and develop a more positive outlook.

Furthermore, practicing self-compassion is crucial in cultivating a positive mindset. It involves treating ourselves with kindness, understanding, and forgiveness, especially during challenging times. By embracing self-compassion, we can counter negative self-talk and build a supportive inner dialogue that encourages growth and self-care.

In conclusion, cultivating a positive mindset is an integral part of self-care. It empowers individuals to navigate life's challenges with resilience, optimism, and hope. By practicing self-awareness, gratitude, affirmations, and self-compassion, we can foster a positive mindset that contributes to our overall well-being and personal growth. Remember, self-care starts from within, and a positive mindset is the key to unlocking its transformative power.

Engaging in Continuous Learning and Growth

In today's fast-paced world, it is more important than ever to prioritize self-care and personal growth. However, many of us neglect this essential aspect of our lives, leading to imbalances and a sense of dissatisfaction. This subchapter aims to shed light on the significance of continuous learning and growth in nurturing oneself and finding true fulfillment.

Self-care is not just about pampering ourselves with occasional treats or indulgences; it is a holistic approach to nurturing our physical, mental, and emotional well-being. Engaging in continuous learning and growth plays a crucial role in this process. By actively seeking knowledge and personal development, we open ourselves up to new opportunities, perspectives, and experiences.

One of the key benefits of continuous learning is the expansion of our horizons. It allows us to step out of our comfort zones and gain a deeper understanding of the world around us. Whether it's through reading books, attending workshops, or pursuing higher education, each new piece of knowledge we acquire helps us grow as individuals. It broadens our perspectives, challenges our preconceived notions, and encourages us to think critically.

Furthermore, continuous learning fuels personal growth by enhancing our skills and abilities. Whether it's learning a new language, acquiring technical expertise, or honing interpersonal skills, each new skill we develop enriches our lives. Not only does it boost our self-confidence and self-esteem, but it also opens up new opportunities for career advancement and personal success.

In addition to the practical benefits, continuous learning also fosters a sense of fulfillment and purpose. When we engage in personal growth, we feel a renewed sense of motivation and drive. We become more self-aware, understanding our strengths, weaknesses, and passions. This self-awareness allows us to set meaningful goals and work towards them with dedication and enthusiasm.

Ultimately, engaging in continuous learning and growth is not just a luxury; it is essential for our overall well-being. It helps us navigate life's challenges, adapt to new circumstances, and remain resilient in the face of adversity. By prioritizing self-care and personal growth, we can transform our lives from a state of neglect to one of nurturing and fulfillment.

So, no matter who you are, whether you are a student, a professional, or a homemaker, recognize the importance of engaging in continuous learning and growth. Embrace the journey towards self-care and personal development, and you will find yourself leading a more fulfilling and meaningful life.

Social Self-Care

In our fast-paced and interconnected world, it is easy to get caught up in the demands of daily life and neglect our own well-being. We often prioritize work, family, and other responsibilities, forgetting to take care of one essential aspect of our lives - our social well-being. This subchapter explores the importance of social self-care and how nurturing our social connections can greatly enhance our overall well-being.

Humans are social beings, and we thrive when we have meaningful connections with others. However, in our busy lives, we sometimes forget to prioritize social interactions and underestimate their impact on our mental and emotional health. Social self-care involves intentionally fostering and nurturing these connections, which can lead to increased happiness, reduced stress levels, and improved overall life satisfaction.

One of the key aspects of social self-care is building and maintaining strong relationships. This includes cultivating friendships, spending quality time with loved ones, and actively participating in social activities. Engaging in activities that bring us joy and allow us to connect with others can have a profound impact on our mental and emotional well-being. Whether it's joining a book club, volunteering for a cause we are passionate about, or simply having regular coffee dates with friends, these interactions can provide a sense of belonging and support that is essential for our overall happiness.

Additionally, social self-care involves setting healthy boundaries in our relationships. It is important to surround ourselves with people who uplift and support us, while also being mindful of toxic or draining relationships that can negatively impact our well-being. Learning to say no when necessary and prioritizing our own needs in social interactions is crucial for maintaining a healthy balance in our lives.

In the digital age, it is also important to be mindful of our social media usage. While social media can be a great tool for staying connected, it can also be a source of comparison and negative self-perception. Taking breaks from social media and engaging in face-to-face interactions can greatly improve our social well-being.

In conclusion, social self-care is an essential aspect of overall well-being. By intentionally nurturing our social connections, setting healthy boundaries, and being mindful of our social media usage, we can enhance our happiness, reduce stress, and cultivate a sense of belonging. So, let us prioritize our social well-being and make time for meaningful connections, for they play a vital role in our journey towards self-care.

Building and Maintaining Supportive Relationships

In our journey towards self-care, building and maintaining supportive relationships plays a crucial role. These relationships not only provide us with emotional support but also contribute to our overall well-being. Whether it is our family, friends, or a significant other, supportive relationships can help us navigate through life's challenges and enhance our ability to practice self-care effectively.

One of the key aspects of building supportive relationships is communication. Good communication fosters understanding, empathy, and trust, which are the foundation stones of nurturing relationships. It is important to express our needs, concerns, and emotions openly, while also actively listening to others. By doing so, we create an environment where both parties feel heard and valued, strengthening the bond between them.

Supportive relationships also require effort and commitment. It is essential to invest time and energy in nurturing these relationships, just as we invest in our own self-care. This can involve spending quality time together, engaging in meaningful conversations, and providing support during challenging times. By being present and available for our loved ones, we not only maintain the relationship but also contribute to their well-being.

Additionally, it is crucial to surround ourselves with people who uplift and inspire us. Negative and toxic relationships can drain our energy and hinder our progress towards self-care. Identifying and distancing ourselves from such relationships is an act of self-care in itself. Instead, seek out individuals who share similar values, goals, and interests.

These individuals will not only support our self-care journey but also provide a positive influence and encouragement along the way.

Furthermore, building and maintaining supportive relationships also involves reciprocity. It is a two-way street, where we both give and receive support. Offering our support to others creates a sense of purpose and fulfillment, while also building trust and strengthening the relationship. Additionally, being open to receiving support when needed allows us to practice self-care without feeling guilty or overwhelmed.

In conclusion, building and maintaining supportive relationships is an integral part of our self-care journey. Through effective communication, commitment, and surrounding ourselves with positive influences, we can enhance our well-being and create a supportive network that uplifts and nurtures us. Remember, self-care is not a solitary pursuit; it thrives in the presence of supportive relationships with our loved ones.

Setting Healthy Boundaries in Social Interactions

In our journey towards self-care, one crucial aspect that often gets neglected is setting healthy boundaries in our social interactions. Boundaries act as a protective shield, ensuring that our emotional, mental, and physical wellbeing is not compromised. They define the limits of what we are comfortable with and help us establish healthy and respectful relationships with others. Without these boundaries, we may find ourselves feeling drained, overwhelmed, and unable to prioritize our own needs.

In today's fast-paced and interconnected world, it is easy to get caught up in the demands and expectations of others. We may feel obligated to say yes to every invitation, take on extra responsibilities, or sacrifice our own well-being to accommodate others. However, it is essential to recognize that setting boundaries is not a selfish act; it is an act of self-preservation and self-respect.

When we set healthy boundaries, we are sending a clear message to ourselves and others that our needs matter. It is about identifying what makes us feel comfortable and secure in our relationships and asserting our right to maintain those boundaries. By doing so, we cultivate a sense of empowerment and regain control over our lives.

To begin setting healthy boundaries, it is crucial to identify our limits and communicate them effectively. This involves understanding our own needs, desires, and values. Reflect on what is important to you and what you are comfortable with. Be honest with yourself about what drains your energy and what brings you joy. Once you have a clear understanding of your limits, communicate them assertively and respectfully to others.

It is important to remember that boundaries are not fixed; they can evolve and change as our needs and circumstances change. Regularly reassessing and adjusting our boundaries is an ongoing process that allows us to grow and adapt while maintaining our self-care practices.

Setting healthy boundaries also means learning to say no without guilt or shame. It is essential to recognize that saying no is not a rejection of others; it is an affirmation of our own needs and priorities. By learning to say no, we free ourselves from unnecessary obligations and create space for activities and relationships that truly nourish us.

In conclusion, setting healthy boundaries in social interactions is a vital aspect of self-care. It allows us to prioritize our own needs, maintain healthy relationships, and cultivate a sense of empowerment. By understanding our limits, communicating them effectively, and learning to say no when necessary, we create a foundation for a fulfilling and balanced life. Remember, setting boundaries is not a selfish act; it is an act of self-love and self-respect.

Chapter 4: Overcoming Challenges

Dealing with Guilt and Self-Sabotage

Guilt and self-sabotage are common obstacles that prevent many individuals from practicing self-care effectively. In this subchapter, we will explore how guilt can hinder our journey towards self-nurturing and provide strategies to overcome self-sabotaging behaviors.

Guilt often arises when we prioritize our own needs over those of others. Society has ingrained in us the belief that self-care is selfish or indulgent. However, it is crucial to understand that self-care is not a luxury but a necessity for our overall well-being. By neglecting our own needs, we risk becoming physically and emotionally exhausted, which ultimately hampers our ability to care for others effectively.

To overcome guilt, we must reframe our mindset and understand that self-care is not only beneficial for ourselves but also for those around us. By taking care of our own physical and mental health, we become better equipped to support and nurture others. Remember, self-care is not an act of selfishness; it is an act of self-preservation and empowerment.

Self-sabotage is another barrier to effective self-care. It stems from deep-seated beliefs that we are unworthy or undeserving of happiness and well-being. These beliefs often manifest in self-destructive behaviors such as procrastination, negative self-talk, or engaging in harmful habits. Recognizing and addressing these self-sabotaging behaviors is essential to break free from their grip.

One strategy to combat self-sabotage is through cultivating self-compassion. Acknowledge that you are human and prone to mistakes, but also capable of growth and change. Treat yourself with the same kindness and understanding you would offer a close friend.

Another powerful method is to identify and challenge negative thought patterns. Replace self-limiting beliefs with empowering affirmations and remind yourself of your inherent worthiness. Surround yourself with positive influences and seek support from loved ones or professionals who can guide you through this process.

Remember, self-care is not a one-time achievement; it is a continuous journey. Embrace the fact that setbacks may occur, but they do not define your progress. Celebrate small victories and be patient with yourself as you navigate this transformative path.

In conclusion, guilt and self-sabotage can impede our ability to prioritize self-care effectively. By understanding the importance of self-nurturing and reframing our mindset, we can overcome guilt and break free from self-sabotaging behaviors. Remember, you are deserving of love, care, and well-being. Embrace the journey towards self-care, and watch as it transforms your life for the better.

Recognizing and Challenging Guilt

Guilt is an emotion that can weigh heavily on our hearts and minds. It often stems from our perceived failure to meet certain expectations, whether they come from ourselves or others. In the journey towards self-care, recognizing and challenging guilt is a crucial step towards freeing ourselves from its burdensome grip.

Many of us struggle with guilt, particularly when it comes to prioritizing our own needs and well-being. We may feel guilty for taking time for ourselves, for saying no to others, or for placing our own happiness above the expectations of others. This guilt can lead to a cycle of self-neglect, where we continuously put ourselves last and deny ourselves the care and attention we deserve.

Recognizing guilt is the first step in breaking this cycle. We must learn to identify when guilt is present and acknowledge the underlying reasons behind it. Is the guilt self-imposed, or is it coming from external sources? Are we holding ourselves to unrealistic standards, or are others placing unfair expectations on us? By understanding the roots of our guilt, we can begin to challenge its validity.

Challenging guilt requires a shift in mindset. We must remind ourselves that self-care is not selfish, but rather a necessary component of a healthy and fulfilling life. Taking care of ourselves allows us to show up as our best selves for others, and it is not something to feel guilty about. It is important to remember that we cannot pour from an empty cup - we must prioritize our own well-being in order to be able to care for others effectively.

One powerful technique for challenging guilt is reframing our thoughts. Instead of seeing self-care as an indulgence or a luxury, we can view it as a necessity. We can remind ourselves that we deserve to be happy and healthy, just like anyone else. By reframing our thoughts, we can gradually replace guilt with self-compassion and acceptance.

It is also crucial to set boundaries and communicate our needs to others. We must learn to say no when necessary and let go of the belief that we must always please everyone around us. By establishing clear boundaries, we can protect our time and energy, and ensure that we have the space to prioritize our own self-care.

In conclusion, recognizing and challenging guilt is essential on the journey towards self-care. By understanding the roots of our guilt, reframing our thoughts, setting boundaries, and communicating our needs, we can break free from the cycle of self-neglect and embrace a life of self-care. Remember, self-care is not a luxury; it is an impotence that allows us to lead a fulfilling and balanced life.

Overcoming Self-Sabotaging Thoughts and Behaviors

In our journey towards self-care, one of the biggest obstacles we often face is our own self-sabotaging thoughts and behaviors. These negative patterns can prevent us from nurturing ourselves and reaching our full potential. However, by recognizing and addressing these tendencies, we can break free from their grip and transform our lives.

Self-sabotage can manifest in various ways, such as negative self-talk, procrastination, perfectionism, and self-destructive habits. These behaviors stem from deep-rooted beliefs and fears that hold us back from prioritizing our well-being. The impotence of self-care becomes evident when we continuously neglect ourselves due to these self-sabotaging patterns.

The first step in overcoming self-sabotage is to become aware of our thoughts and behaviors. Start paying attention to the negative narratives running through your mind and the actions that hinder your self-care routine. Journaling can be a powerful tool to record and reflect on these patterns, helping you gain clarity and understanding.

Once you've identified your self-sabotaging thoughts and behaviors, the next step is to challenge and reframe them. Replace negative self-talk with positive affirmations and empowering beliefs. Remind yourself that you deserve self-care and that taking care of yourself is not selfish but necessary for your overall well-being.

Another effective strategy is to set realistic goals and break them down into smaller, achievable steps. Procrastination often stems from feeling overwhelmed or fearing failure. By breaking tasks into manageable chunks, you can reduce anxiety and increase motivation. Celebrate small victories along the way, reinforcing positive behavior and building self-confidence.

It's also crucial to address any underlying emotional issues that contribute to self-sabotage. Seek support from trusted friends, family, or a therapist who can provide guidance and help you navigate these challenges. Developing healthy coping mechanisms, such as meditation, exercise, or creative outlets, can also assist in managing stress and negative emotions.

Remember, overcoming self-sabotage is a process that requires patience and self-compassion. Be kind to yourself during this journey and celebrate every step forward. By actively working to overcome self-sabotaging thoughts and behaviors, you can transform your life and embrace the impotence of self-care. You deserve to nurture yourself and experience the positive impact it can have on your overall well-being.

Overcoming Time Constraints

In today's fast-paced world, time has become a precious commodity. We find ourselves constantly juggling multiple responsibilities, leaving little room for self-care. We often neglect our own well-being in favor of meeting deadlines, fulfilling obligations, and taking care of others. However, it is essential to recognize the importance of self-care and make it a priority in our lives.

The impotence of self-care cannot be overstated. It is not a luxury but a necessity for maintaining our physical, mental, and emotional well-being. Neglecting self-care can lead to burnout, stress, and a decline in overall health. It is crucial to find a balance between our responsibilities and taking care of ourselves.

Overcoming time constraints may seem like a daunting task, but it is possible with some conscious effort and planning. Here are a few strategies to help you prioritize self-care in your busy schedule:

1. Time Management: Start by evaluating how you spend your time. Identify activities that can be minimized or eliminated to create space for self-care. Set realistic goals and allocate specific time slots for self-care activities.

2. Prioritize: Understand that self-care is not selfish; it is necessary for your well-being. Learn to say no to non-essential commitments and make self-care a non-negotiable part of your routine.

3. Break It Down: You don't need to dedicate hours to self-care every day. Break it down into smaller, manageable activities that can be incorporated into your daily routine. It could be as simple as taking a

short walk, practicing deep breathing exercises, or enjoying a hobby for a few minutes.

4. Delegate: Don't hesitate to delegate tasks to others. It is okay to ask for help and share responsibilities. This will free up time for self-care without compromising your other commitments.

5. Mindful Multitasking: Look for opportunities to combine self-care with other activities. For example, listen to a podcast or an audiobook while commuting, or practice mindfulness while doing household chores.

Remember, self-care is not a one-time event; it is an ongoing process. It requires consistent effort and commitment. By overcoming time constraints and prioritizing self-care, you are investing in your own well-being, which will ultimately benefit every aspect of your life.

Take charge of your time and make self-care a non-negotiable part of your daily routine. You deserve it, and your overall well-being depends on it. Start small, be consistent, and watch how self-care transforms your life from neglect to nurturing.

Prioritizing Self-Care in a Busy Schedule

In today's fast-paced world, it's easy to become overwhelmed with the demands of work, family, and other responsibilities. Many of us find ourselves constantly juggling multiple tasks and struggling to find time for ourselves. However, amidst the chaos, it is crucial to prioritize self-care for our overall well-being and happiness. This subchapter explores the importance of self-care and provides practical strategies for incorporating it into our busy schedules.

Self-care is not a luxury; it is a necessity. It encompasses activities that nurture and replenish our physical, mental, and emotional well-being. Neglecting self-care can lead to burnout, decreased productivity, and a decline in our overall quality of life. It is vital to recognize that taking care of ourselves is not selfish but rather a way to ensure we have the energy and resilience needed to fulfill our other commitments.

In a busy schedule, carving out time for self-care may seem daunting. However, it starts with shifting our mindset and making self-care a priority. Begin by acknowledging that you deserve care and setting boundaries to protect your time. Assess your schedule and identify areas where you can make small changes to incorporate self-care.

One effective strategy is to break self-care into smaller, manageable chunks. Instead of thinking you need an entire day or even hours for self-care, focus on finding short pockets of time throughout the day. This could be as simple as taking a short walk during your lunch break, practicing deep breathing exercises, or indulging in a few minutes of your favorite hobby.

Another approach is to incorporate self-care into existing routines. For instance, make your morning routine a mindful ritual by savoring a cup of tea or engaging in a brief meditation. Transform your commute into a time for relaxation by listening to calming music or an inspiring podcast. By integrating self-care into your daily rituals, you can ensure it becomes a regular part of your routine.

Remember, self-care looks different for everyone. It could involve engaging in physical activities, such as exercise or yoga, seeking mental stimulation through reading or learning new skills, or nurturing your emotional well-being by spending time with loved ones or engaging in activities that bring you joy.

Prioritizing self-care in a busy schedule requires intention and commitment. It may involve saying no to certain obligations or delegating tasks to create space for yourself. As you make self-care a non-negotiable part of your life, you will experience increased energy, improved mental clarity, and a greater sense of fulfillment in all areas of your life.

In conclusion, neglecting self-care can have detrimental effects on our physical, mental, and emotional well-being. It is essential to prioritize self-care in a busy schedule to maintain a healthy balance. By making small adjustments, integrating self-care into daily routines, and setting boundaries, we can ensure that self-care becomes a regular practice. Remember, you deserve to take care of yourself – it is not selfish, but rather a way to nurture your overall well-being and live a more fulfilling life.

Finding Creative Ways to Make Time for Self-Care

In today's fast-paced world, it's easy to get caught up in the hustle and bustle of daily life, often neglecting our own well-being. Self-care is crucial for maintaining our mental, emotional, and physical health, yet it is often overlooked or put on the back burner. This subchapter aims to address the importance of self-care and provide creative ways for everyone, regardless of their circumstances, to carve out time for nurturing themselves.

The impotence of self-care cannot be overstated. Taking care of yourself allows you to recharge, reduce stress, and improve overall happiness and productivity. It is not a selfish act, but rather an essential part of maintaining a healthy and balanced life. However, finding time for self-care can be challenging, especially when our schedules are packed with work, family commitments, and other responsibilities.

One creative approach to making time for self-care is to prioritize and schedule it into your day. Treat self-care as an appointment with yourself that cannot be canceled or rescheduled. Set aside a specific time each day, even if it's just 15 minutes, to engage in activities that bring you joy and relaxation. It could be reading a book, practicing yoga, taking a walk in nature, or indulging in a long bath. Whatever it is, make it a non-negotiable part of your routine.

Another creative way to make time for self-care is to involve others. Seek support from your loved ones, friends, or colleagues, and establish a self-care network. Arrange regular meet-ups or outings where you can engage in activities that promote well-being together.

Not only will this help you make time for self-care, but it will also strengthen your relationships and create a sense of community.

Additionally, consider incorporating self-care into your daily tasks. For example, while commuting to work, listen to relaxing music or an uplifting podcast. During your lunch break, take a mindful walk or practice deep breathing exercises. By infusing self-care into your existing routine, you can make the most of the time you already have.

Remember that self-care doesn't have to be time-consuming or expensive. It's about finding small moments throughout the day to nourish yourself. Whether it's sipping a cup of tea, journaling, or meditating, even brief moments of self-care can have a profound impact on your well-being.

In conclusion, self-care is a vital aspect of leading a fulfilling and balanced life. By prioritizing and creatively making time for self-care, you can ensure your own well-being and improve your ability to navigate life's challenges. Remember, you deserve to be nurtured, and finding creative ways to make time for self-care will bring you one step closer to a happier, healthier you.

Seeking Support and Accountability

In our journey towards self-care, one of the most critical aspects often overlooked is the importance of seeking support and accountability. We live in a fast-paced world where self-care has become a neglected concept for many individuals. However, acknowledging the impotence of self-care and actively seeking support and accountability can transform our lives in unimaginable ways.

Self-care is not a solitary endeavor; it requires a community of individuals who can support and uplift us on our path. By surrounding ourselves with like-minded people who understand the significance of self-care, we create an environment that encourages personal growth and resilience. These individuals can be our friends, family members, or even support groups specifically designed to foster self-care practices.

One of the primary reasons why self-care often fails is the lack of accountability. We may have the best intentions when it comes to taking care of ourselves, but without someone to hold us accountable, we often fall back into old patterns and neglect our own well-being. By seeking accountability, we empower ourselves to stay committed to self-care routines and make it a priority in our lives.

There are numerous ways to seek support and accountability on our self-care journey. Joining a self-care community or finding an accountability partner can provide the necessary encouragement and motivation to stay on track. Sharing our goals and aspirations with others not only holds us accountable but also allows us to receive valuable feedback and advice from those who have experienced similar challenges.

Additionally, seeking professional support can be immensely beneficial. Therapists, life coaches, or wellness practitioners can provide guidance on self-care techniques, help us identify self-destructive patterns, and offer strategies to overcome obstacles and setbacks. These professionals are trained to understand the intricacies of self-care and can provide tailored solutions that resonate with our unique circumstances.

Furthermore, technology has made it easier than ever to access support and accountability. Online communities, forums, and apps dedicated to self-care are abundant. These platforms offer a virtual support system where individuals from all walks of life can connect, share experiences, and hold each other accountable.

In conclusion, seeking support and accountability is vital on our journey towards self-care. Recognizing the impotence of self-care is the first step, but actively pursuing a network of individuals who can provide support and hold us accountable is equally crucial. By surrounding ourselves with like-minded people, seeking professional guidance, and utilizing technology, we can create a robust support system that empowers us to prioritize self-care and ultimately transform our lives for the better. Remember, self-care is not a solitary endeavor, and together we can nurture ourselves and create a more fulfilling and balanced life.

Identifying Sources of Support

In our journey towards self-care, one of the most important steps we can take is to identify and utilize the sources of support available to us. Often, we may feel overwhelmed or unsure of where to turn when we are in need of assistance. However, by recognizing the various resources around us, we can empower ourselves to overcome challenges and nurture our well-being.

Support can come in many forms, and it is crucial to remember that we are not alone in this journey. The first step in identifying sources of support is to acknowledge the importance of self-care. All too often, we neglect our own needs and prioritize the demands of others. However, by understanding the impotence of self-care, we can start to make a change and seek support.

One valuable source of support is our personal network of family and friends. These individuals can provide emotional support, lend a listening ear, and offer advice or guidance. Sharing our struggles and concerns with loved ones can lighten our burdens and help us gain new perspectives. It is important to cultivate these relationships and reach out when we need assistance.

Another potential source of support is professional help. Seeking therapy or counseling can provide a safe space to explore our emotions, develop coping strategies, and gain insights into our own patterns and behaviors. Mental health professionals are trained to provide guidance and support, and they can offer valuable tools for self-care.

Furthermore, there are numerous community resources available that can support our journey towards self-care. These may include support groups, workshops, or organizations focused on specific areas of concern, such as addiction recovery, stress management, or self-esteem building. Engaging with like-minded individuals who have experienced similar challenges can provide a sense of belonging and validation, while also offering practical advice and support.

Lastly, technology has opened up new avenues for support. Online communities, forums, and social media groups can connect us with individuals facing similar issues, even if we are physically isolated. These virtual spaces can provide a sense of camaraderie, advice, and encouragement.

In conclusion, identifying sources of support is a crucial aspect of our journey towards self-care. By recognizing the importance of self-care and reaching out for assistance, we can cultivate a network of support that will help us navigate life's challenges. Whether it be through our personal relationships, professional help, community resources, or online platforms, we can find the support we need to nurture ourselves and live a more fulfilling life. Remember, you are not alone - there is support available to you, and you are deserving of the care and attention you give to others.

Creating Accountability Systems

Accountability is a crucial aspect of self-care that is often overlooked. Many of us struggle with neglecting our own well-being due to various reasons, such as a lack of time, energy, or understanding of its importance. However, incorporating accountability systems into our lives can greatly enhance our ability to prioritize self-care and lead to a more fulfilling and balanced lifestyle.

One of the most effective ways to create accountability systems is by setting goals and creating a plan to achieve them. This involves identifying specific areas of self-care that require attention and establishing clear objectives for improvement. Whether it's taking care of your physical health, mental well-being, or nurturing your relationships, having defined goals helps you stay focused and motivated.

To ensure accountability, it is essential to establish measurable targets and timelines. For example, if your goal is to improve your physical health, you can set specific targets for exercise frequency, healthy eating habits, and weight management. By tracking your progress and monitoring your achievements regularly, you can hold yourself accountable for reaching these milestones.

In addition to personal accountability, involving others in your self-care journey can greatly enhance your commitment. Share your goals and plans with a trusted friend, family member, or mentor who can provide support and hold you accountable. Regular check-ins and discussions about progress can help you stay on track and provide an external perspective on your self-care efforts.

Another effective accountability system is creating a visual representation of your goals, such as a vision board or a daily tracker. Having a tangible reminder of your aspirations can serve as a powerful motivator and reinforcement of your commitment to self-care. Place it somewhere visible, like your desk or bedroom wall, to serve as a constant reminder of your priorities.

Moreover, technology can be a valuable tool for accountability. There are numerous apps and online platforms available that can help you track your progress, set reminders, and even connect with like-minded individuals who are also on a self-care journey. Utilizing these resources can provide additional support and accountability in your pursuit of well-being.

Ultimately, creating accountability systems is crucial for overcoming the neglect of self-care. By setting goals, establishing measurable targets, involving others, and utilizing technology, you can ensure that self-care remains a priority in your life. Remember, self-care is not selfish; it is a necessary practice that enables you to nurture yourself so that you can better care for others. Start building your accountability systems today and embark on a journey towards a healthier, more fulfilling life.

Chapter 5: Sustaining Self-Care Practices

Creating a Self-Care Plan

In today's fast-paced and demanding world, it is easy to overlook the importance of taking care of ourselves. We often find ourselves caught up in the daily grind, neglecting our physical, mental, and emotional well-being. However, prioritizing self-care is not just a luxury; it is an essential aspect of leading a balanced and fulfilling life. In this subchapter, we will explore the significance of self-care and guide you through the process of creating a personalized self-care plan.

Self-care is not a selfish act; it is a necessary practice that allows us to recharge, rejuvenate, and maintain our overall health and well-being. Neglecting self-care can lead to burnout, increased stress levels, and a decline in our physical and mental health. It is crucial to recognize that we cannot pour from an empty cup. By making ourselves a priority and investing time and energy into self-care, we are better equipped to handle life's challenges and responsibilities.

To create a self-care plan, it is essential to first assess your needs and identify the areas in which you may be neglecting yourself. Start by reflecting on your physical, mental, and emotional well-being. Are you getting enough sleep? Are you engaging in activities that bring you joy and fulfillment? Are you taking care of your physical health through exercise and a balanced diet? These are just a few questions to consider when evaluating your self-care needs.

Once you have identified your areas of neglect, it is time to take action. Begin by setting realistic goals that align with your self-care needs.

These goals can range from incorporating regular exercise into your routine to dedicating time for relaxation and mindfulness practices. Remember, self-care is not a one-size-fits-all approach, so tailor your plan to your individual preferences and interests.

Next, establish a routine that allows for regular self-care activities. This may involve scheduling specific times in your calendar or setting reminders to prioritize self-care. It is essential to treat your self-care activities with the same level of commitment and importance as you would any other appointment or responsibility.

Lastly, be kind to yourself and allow for flexibility in your self-care plan. Life can be unpredictable, and there may be times when your plan needs to be adjusted. Embrace self-compassion and make modifications as needed, ensuring that self-care remains a consistent part of your life.

Remember, self-care is not a luxury; it is a necessity. By creating a personalized self-care plan, you are taking the first step towards nurturing yourself and leading a more balanced and fulfilling life. Embrace the impotence of self-care and embark on this journey towards self-nurturing today.

Setting Realistic Goals

In the fast-paced world we live in today, it is easy to get caught up in the hustle and bustle of everyday life and neglect our own well-being. We often prioritize our professional commitments, familial responsibilities, and social obligations, leaving little time and energy to take care of ourselves. However, it is essential to understand the impotence of self-care and the importance of setting realistic goals to achieve a healthier and more fulfilling life.

Self-care is not a luxury; it is a necessity for our overall well-being. It involves consciously taking care of our physical, mental, and emotional health. However, many of us struggle with neglecting our own needs and putting ourselves last on the priority list. This neglect can lead to feelings of burnout, stress, and a general sense of unhappiness. Therefore, it is crucial to understand the significance of self-care and the role it plays in our lives.

One of the key aspects of self-care is setting realistic goals. Often, we set unrealistic expectations for ourselves, leading to disappointment and frustration when we are unable to achieve them. Setting realistic goals allows us to break our larger aspirations into smaller, more manageable steps. This approach not only increases our chances of success but also helps us maintain our motivation and momentum.

When setting goals, it is essential to be specific and measurable. Instead of setting a vague goal like "I want to exercise more," try setting a specific goal like "I will go for a 30-minute walk three times a week." This specificity helps us track our progress and provides a sense of accomplishment when we achieve our goals.

Additionally, it is crucial to set goals that align with our values and priorities. Reflect on what truly matters to you and what brings you joy and fulfillment. Setting goals that are meaningful to you will help you stay motivated and committed to achieving them.

Moreover, it is important to be flexible and adaptable when setting goals. Life is unpredictable, and circumstances may change. Being open to adjusting our goals when necessary allows us to stay on track and overcome any obstacles that may arise.

In conclusion, understanding the impotence of self-care is vital for everyone. Setting realistic goals is a crucial component of self-care as it allows us to prioritize our well-being and achieve a healthier, more balanced life. By setting specific, measurable, and meaningful goals, we can chart a path towards self-nurturing and ultimately experience a greater sense of fulfillment and happiness. Remember, self-care is not selfish; it is an investment in our overall well-being.

Designing a Personalized Self-Care Routine

Self-care is an essential aspect of our well-being, yet it is often neglected in the hustle and bustle of our daily lives. Taking care of ourselves is not a luxury but a necessity that allows us to thrive in all areas of our lives. In this subchapter, we will explore the importance of self-care and guide you on how to design a personalized self-care routine that suits your unique needs.

The Impotence of Self-Care

In today's fast-paced world, many of us tend to prioritize the needs of others over our own. We often neglect our physical, mental, and emotional well-being, thinking that it can wait or that it is selfish to focus on ourselves. However, neglecting self-care can lead to burnout, decreased productivity, and a decline in overall happiness.

Self-care is not just about pampering ourselves with bubble baths or indulging in guilty pleasures. It encompasses a broader range of activities that nourish our mind, body, and soul. It involves setting boundaries, practicing self-compassion, and engaging in activities that bring us joy and fulfillment.

Designing Your Personalized Self-Care Routine

Creating a personalized self-care routine requires reflection and experimentation. Start by identifying the areas of your life that need attention and improvement. Are you neglecting your physical health, emotional well-being, or relationships? Once you have identified the areas that require nurturing, you can begin designing a routine that addresses these specific needs.

Consider your preferences and interests when selecting self-care activities. Some people find solace in physical activities like yoga or jogging, while others prefer artistic expressions such as painting or writing. Experiment with different activities to discover what resonates with you the most.

Establish a daily, weekly, or monthly schedule for your self-care routine. Set aside dedicated time for self-care activities and treat them as non-negotiable appointments with yourself. Remember that self-care is not a one-time event but an ongoing practice that requires consistency and commitment.

Keep in mind that self-care is not a selfish act. By taking care of yourself, you are better equipped to care for others and fulfill your responsibilities. Embrace the fact that you deserve love, care, and attention just as much as anyone else.

In conclusion, designing a personalized self-care routine is crucial for our overall well-being. By recognizing the importance of self-care and dedicating time to nurture ourselves, we can lead happier, more fulfilling lives. So, take the first step today and embark on a journey towards self-care. You deserve it.

Cultivating Resilience and Adaptability

Resilience and adaptability are key qualities that can help individuals navigate the challenges and uncertainties of life. In the context of self-care, these qualities are essential for maintaining a healthy and balanced lifestyle. In this subchapter, we will explore the importance of cultivating resilience and adaptability and how these traits can contribute to an individual's overall well-being.

Resilience refers to the ability to bounce back from difficult experiences or setbacks. It is the capacity to remain emotionally stable and mentally strong in the face of adversity. When it comes to self-care, resilience plays a crucial role in maintaining a positive mindset and overcoming obstacles that may hinder one's well-being. By cultivating resilience, individuals can develop a greater sense of self-confidence and belief in their ability to overcome challenges and take charge of their own lives.

Adaptability, on the other hand, refers to the ability to adjust to new circumstances and changes. In today's fast-paced and ever-changing world, being adaptable is essential for personal growth and self-care. Adaptable individuals are more likely to embrace change, learn from new experiences, and find creative solutions to problems. They are open to trying new things and are not easily discouraged when faced with unfamiliar situations. By cultivating adaptability, individuals can become more resilient and better equipped to handle the ups and downs of life.

So, how can one cultivate resilience and adaptability? It starts with developing a growth mindset – the belief that challenges and setbacks are opportunities for learning and growth. This mindset encourages individuals to view obstacles as temporary roadblocks rather than insurmountable barriers. It also involves building a strong support system of family, friends, and mentors who can provide guidance and encouragement during difficult times.

Additionally, practicing self-compassion is vital in cultivating resilience and adaptability. Treating oneself with kindness, understanding, and forgiveness allows individuals to bounce back from setbacks with a renewed sense of purpose and determination. Engaging in regular self-care activities such as exercise, meditation, and pursuing hobbies can also contribute to building resilience and adaptability.

In conclusion, cultivating resilience and adaptability is paramount for individuals seeking to prioritize self-care. These qualities enable individuals to navigate life's challenges with grace and resilience. By embracing change, maintaining a growth mindset, and practicing self-compassion, one can develop the inner strength and flexibility necessary for overall well-being. So, let us embark on a journey towards self-care, nurturing our resilience and adaptability, and creating a fulfilling and balanced life for ourselves.

Embracing Change and Uncertainty

Change is an inevitable part of life, and uncertainty often accompanies it. As human beings, we often find ourselves resistant to change and uncomfortable with the unknown. However, in the journey towards self-care, embracing change and uncertainty is crucial. It is through these experiences that we can truly grow and nurture ourselves.

Change can be both exciting and daunting. It pushes us out of our comfort zones and challenges us to adapt. By embracing change, we open ourselves up to new opportunities and possibilities. We learn to let go of what no longer serves us and make room for personal growth. Whether it is a change in career, relationships, or even our own mindset, each step towards embracing change brings us closer to self-care.

Uncertainty, on the other hand, can be unsettling. We crave stability and predictability, but life often has other plans. It is during times of uncertainty that our self-care practices become even more important. Instead of resisting uncertainty, we can learn to embrace it as a catalyst for personal transformation. By letting go of the need for control and surrendering to the unknown, we open ourselves up to new perspectives and possibilities.

Embracing change and uncertainty requires a shift in mindset. Instead of fearing the unknown, we can view it as an opportunity for growth and self-discovery. It is a chance to explore our strengths, values, and desires. By embracing change, we can break free from the shackles of routine and embark on a journey of self-care and self-fulfillment.

In the book "From Neglect to Nurturing: A Journey Towards Self-Care," we delve into the importance of embracing change and uncertainty. Through personal stories, practical exercises, and insightful advice, we guide readers towards a deeper understanding of the impotence of self-care. We explore how embracing change can lead to personal transformation and how uncertainty can be a catalyst for self-discovery.

This subchapter is addressed to everyone, as the impotence of self-care knows no boundaries. Whether you are a young professional navigating the challenges of a changing world, a parent juggling multiple responsibilities, or a retiree seeking new purpose, embracing change and uncertainty is essential for your well-being. By embracing the unknown and nurturing ourselves through self-care practices, we can navigate life's uncertainties with grace and resilience.

In conclusion, embracing change and uncertainty is a vital aspect of our journey towards self-care. By letting go of fear and resistance, we open ourselves up to personal growth and transformation. In the book "From Neglect to Nurturing: A Journey Towards Self-Care," we explore the impotence of self-care in the face of change and uncertainty. It is through embracing these experiences that we can truly nurture ourselves and create a more fulfilling life.

Developing Coping Mechanisms for Stressful Situations

In our fast-paced and demanding world, stress has become an inevitable part of our lives. From work pressures to personal challenges, stress can take a toll on our mental and physical well-being. However, it is crucial to recognize the impotence of self-care in managing and alleviating stress. In this subchapter, we will delve into the importance of developing coping mechanisms for stressful situations and explore practical strategies to nurture our well-being.

The first step towards developing coping mechanisms is to identify the sources of stress in our lives. It could be a demanding job, relationship issues, financial burdens, or health concerns. By understanding the root causes, we can work towards finding effective ways to cope with them. This self-awareness empowers us to take control of our stress levels and make positive changes.

One of the most effective coping mechanisms is cultivating a healthy lifestyle. Regular exercise, a balanced diet, and sufficient sleep play a vital role in reducing stress. Engaging in physical activities not only helps release endorphins, the feel-good hormones, but also provides an outlet for pent-up emotions. Additionally, consuming nutritious foods and getting enough rest strengthens our resilience to stressors.

Another powerful coping mechanism is incorporating relaxation techniques into our daily routine. Deep breathing exercises, meditation, and mindfulness practices can help calm the mind and promote a sense of inner peace. These techniques allow us to focus on the present moment, letting go of worries and anxieties.

Furthermore, building a support network is crucial for managing stress. Surrounding ourselves with positive and understanding individuals can offer emotional support and practical advice. Sharing our feelings and concerns with trusted friends, family, or even seeking professional help can provide valuable insights and help us gain a fresh perspective.

Lastly, self-care activities should be prioritized to manage stress effectively. Engaging in hobbies, pursuing creative outlets, or spending time in nature can all contribute to our overall well-being. By dedicating time to activities that bring us joy and relaxation, we can replenish our energy and build resilience against stress.

In conclusion, developing coping mechanisms for stressful situations is of utmost importance in our journey towards self-care. By identifying the sources of stress, adopting a healthy lifestyle, practicing relaxation techniques, building a support network, and indulging in self-care activities, we can effectively manage stress and nurture our well-being. Remember, self-care is not a luxury but a necessity to lead a fulfilling and balanced life.

Celebrating Self-Care Victories

Subchapter: Celebrating Self-Care Victories

Introduction:
In our relentless pursuit of success and happiness, we often neglect the most important aspect of our lives – ourselves. We neglect self-care, unaware of its profound impact on our physical, mental, and emotional well-being. This subchapter, titled "Celebrating Self-Care Victories," is a testament to the importance and impotence of self-care in our lives. It serves as a reminder to everyone that nurturing ourselves is not only essential but also a cause for celebration.

Recognizing the Impotence of Self-Care:
Before we can celebrate our victories, it is crucial to understand the impotence of self-care. Self-care goes beyond occasional treats or indulgences; it is a fundamental practice that allows us to flourish. It empowers us to prioritize our own needs, set boundaries, and cultivate a healthy relationship with ourselves. Neglecting self-care can lead to burnout, decreased productivity, and a diminished sense of self-worth. By acknowledging its significance, we can embark on a transformative journey towards self-nurturing.

The Journey Towards Self-Care Victories:
Embarking on a journey towards self-care is not always easy. We might face obstacles, internal resistance, or societal pressures that discourage us from putting ourselves first. However, every small step we take towards self-care is a victory worth celebrating.

Discovering Self-Care Rituals:
One of the keys to self-care victories is discovering and implementing

personalized self-care rituals. These rituals can range from simple acts of self-compassion, such as taking regular breaks, practicing mindfulness, or engaging in hobbies, to more profound transformations, like reevaluating our priorities, adopting healthier lifestyles, or seeking professional help. Each individual's journey is unique, and it is essential to find what resonates with us personally.

Overcoming Barriers:
As we embark on our self-care journey, we must also address the barriers that hinder our progress. This may include societal expectations, guilt, or the misconception that self-care is selfish. By challenging these barriers, we can empower ourselves to prioritize our well-being and celebrate the victories that come along the way.

Celebrating Self-Care Victories:
Finally, it is crucial to acknowledge and celebrate our self-care victories. These victories can be both big and small – from consistently practicing self-care rituals to achieving significant milestones in our well-being journey. By celebrating these triumphs, we reinforce the importance of self-care in our lives and inspire others to prioritize themselves as well.

Conclusion:
Self-care is a transformative journey that requires dedication, self-compassion, and the willingness to celebrate our victories. By understanding the impotence of self-care and embarking on this journey, we nurture ourselves, reclaim our well-being, and inspire others to do the same. Let us all celebrate our self-care victories and create a world where nurturing ourselves is not only accepted but also cherished.

Recognizing and Acknowledging Progress

In our journey towards self-care, it is crucial to recognize and acknowledge the progress we make along the way. Often, we tend to focus on our failures and shortcomings, overlooking the small victories and advancements we achieve on a daily basis. This subchapter aims to shed light on the importance of recognizing and acknowledging our progress in nurturing ourselves, no matter how small or insignificant it may seem.

Self-care is not a destination; it is a continuous process that requires patience and perseverance. It is easy to become disheartened when faced with setbacks or challenges, but by recognizing and acknowledging the progress we have already made, we can find the motivation to keep moving forward.

Each person's journey towards self-care is unique, and comparing ourselves to others can be detrimental to our progress. Instead, we need to focus on our personal growth and celebrate the steps we have taken towards nurturing ourselves. This can be as simple as honoring the moments when we prioritize our well-being over other obligations or acknowledging the positive changes we have made in our habits and mindset.

By recognizing our progress, we cultivate a sense of self-worth and confidence. It helps us to believe in our capabilities and reinforces the idea that we are worthy of the time and effort it takes to care for ourselves. Moreover, acknowledging our progress allows us to reflect on the strategies and actions that have worked well for us, enabling us to refine our self-care routines and make further progress.

In the journey towards self-care, no progress is too small to be acknowledged. Whether it is practicing mindfulness for a few minutes each day, setting boundaries with toxic individuals, or seeking professional help when needed, every step forward is significant. Embracing the progress we have made, no matter how incremental, creates a positive mindset and fuels our motivation to continue nurturing ourselves.

Remember, self-care is not a race or a competition. It is about acknowledging our efforts, no matter how big or small, and celebrating our growth. Each small victory is a testament to our commitment to self-improvement and a reminder that we are capable of making positive changes in our lives. So, take a moment to recognize and acknowledge your progress, for it is through these small steps that we can transform neglect into nurturing and embark on a fulfilling journey towards self-care.

Rewarding Yourself for Consistent Self-Care Efforts

In the hustle and bustle of everyday life, it is easy to neglect our own well-being. We often prioritize work, family, and other responsibilities, leaving little time for self-care. However, as we navigate through the challenges of life, it becomes increasingly evident that neglecting our own needs can lead to burnout, resentment, and a decline in overall mental and physical health.

Recognizing the impotence of self-care is the first step towards achieving a healthier and more balanced life. Self-care goes beyond bubble baths and indulging in guilty pleasures; it is a comprehensive approach to nurturing ourselves physically, emotionally, and spiritually. It encompasses activities that recharge our energy, reduce stress, and promote personal growth.

Consistency is key when it comes to self-care. It is not a one-time event or a quick fix; it is a continuous and conscious effort to prioritize our well-being. Engaging in self-care activities on a regular basis can help us maintain a positive mindset, improve our relationships, and boost our productivity. However, many of us struggle to stay consistent in our self-care efforts. We often find ourselves prioritizing the needs of others or succumbing to feelings of guilt when we take time for ourselves.

To overcome these challenges and stay motivated in our self-care journey, it is essential to reward ourselves for consistent efforts. Rewards act as positive reinforcement, encouraging us to continue prioritizing our well-being. They serve as a reminder that self-care is not selfish but necessary for our overall happiness and fulfillment.

When it comes to rewarding yourself for consistent self-care efforts, there are countless options. It is important to choose rewards that resonate with you personally and align with your interests and values. It could be something as simple as treating yourself to a favorite meal, taking a day off to engage in a hobby, or splurging on a well-deserved vacation. The key is to make the reward meaningful to you, so it truly feels like a pat on the back for your dedication to self-care.

Remember, self-care is not a luxury; it is a fundamental necessity for a healthy and balanced life. By rewarding yourself for consistent self-care efforts, you are reinforcing the importance of prioritizing your well-being. So, take a moment to reflect on your self-care journey, set achievable goals, and reward yourself along the way. You deserve it!

Conclusion: Embracing a Life of Self-Care

Congratulations! By reaching the conclusion of this book, you have taken an important step towards prioritizing your well-being. In our fast-paced and demanding world, self-care often gets overlooked, causing negative consequences for our physical, mental, and emotional health. However, by embracing a life of self-care, you can reclaim your power and create a happier, healthier, and more fulfilling existence.

Throughout this journey, we have explored the impotence of self-care, understanding that it is not a luxury, but a necessity. We have delved into the reasons why neglecting self-care can lead to burnout, stress, and a diminished quality of life. We have also explored the various aspects of self-care, including physical, emotional, mental, and spiritual well-being, and how they are all interconnected.

It is essential to recognize that self-care is not selfish. By taking care of yourself, you are better equipped to care for others and fulfill your responsibilities. It is like the metaphorical oxygen mask on an airplane – you must secure your own mask before assisting others. Similarly, prioritizing self-care enables you to show up as the best version of yourself in all areas of your life.

Embracing a life of self-care requires making intentional choices and setting boundaries. It means carving out time for activities that bring you joy, nourish your soul, and rejuvenate your spirit. It means saying no to things that drain your energy and learning to delegate tasks when necessary. It means cultivating self-compassion and practicing self-acceptance, understanding that you are worthy of love and care.

Remember, self-care is not a one-time event; it is a lifelong journey. It requires consistency, commitment, and a willingness to adapt as your needs evolve. It may take time to establish new habits, but the rewards are immeasurable – increased energy, improved relationships, enhanced creativity, and a greater sense of fulfillment.

As you embark on this path of self-care, surround yourself with a supportive community that understands the importance of prioritizing well-being. Seek out resources, such as books, workshops, or online communities, that can provide guidance and inspiration. Remember, you are not alone in this journey – there are countless others who are also striving to embrace a life of self-care.

In conclusion, by embracing a life of self-care, you are taking a powerful step towards reclaiming your happiness and well-being. Remember to be gentle with yourself, celebrate your progress, and continue to prioritize self-care as an act of self-love. You deserve it, and the world needs you at your best.

Begin your journey towards self-care today, and watch as your life transforms into one filled with joy, fulfillment, and a deep sense of purpose.

www.ingramcontent.com/pod-product-compliance
Lightning Source LLC
LaVergne TN
LVHW051954060526
838201LV00059B/3641